HOW I BARELY SURVIVE BEING A STAY-AT-HOME MOM

HELPFUL TIPS TO OVERCOME THE MOM GUILT, LONELINESS, AND DAILY STRUGGLES OF PARENTING, WITH HONESTY & HUMOR

ANDIE KINGBRUM

This book is dedicated to my children. Without them and their daily challenges, I would not have the inspiration to write this book. Addison, Brody, and Brock, keep on challenging me. Surprise me every day, continue to ask me a million questions, and please grow into wonderful humans. You guys keep my head spinning and my heart full. I can't wait until you have children of your own to experience, so I can giggle quietly and remember the daily struggles that you all put me through which made being a mother totally worth it.

CONTENTS

A FREE GIFT FOR MY READERS!

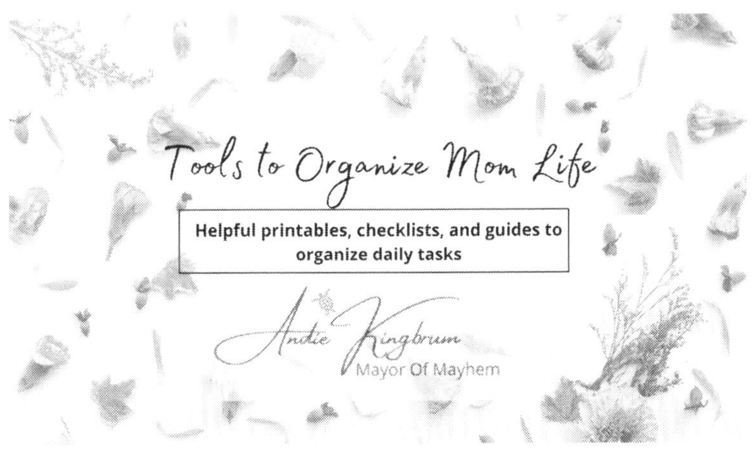

TEN downloadable pages to help fellow parents get organized in daily life. Scan the QR code below to receive your FREE printable tools.

https://themayorofmayhem.activehosted.com/f/1

INTRODUCTION

There I was, at a friend's house, chatting over a glass of wine while the children were wreaking havoc in her basement. We were reminiscing about the most memorable times in our lives being a mother. Our biggest failures so to speak. I was telling her about the time when I let my daughter fall out of her highchair onto her head as a baby. I was nursing my peanut of a daughter every hour on the hour, and I was beyond exhausted. I have never felt that kind of exhaustion before. I was hallucinating and walking into walls. I felt like I was a zombie. A real-life zombie. I had set her in her highchair like I did numerous times a day, this time though I didn't have the tray table on. I turned around to grab her food and I heard a loud thud followed by a terrible scream. I lost it after that. Rushed her to the emergency room by myself mind you, and proceeded to have a panic attack until the next day. She was fine thankfully, but I most definitely was not. I realized then that I am not Mary freaking Poppins and I cannot do everything like the mothers on social media do. So, I called my mom and told her I needed help. She came over and cleaned and did laundry while I napped in between nursing. It was just what I needed.

As we were sitting there chatting I realized that being a mother is hard. I was so tired of seeing all these posts on social media that make parenting sound so easy and perfect. They were all liars I decided. I left every single mothers group I was a part of and followed my gut when it came to raising my kids. I decided that I was going to write a book about my adventures. It is going to be honest and probably great birth control for a teen. I wanted others in my position to know they are not alone and parenting sucks sometimes. When she told me her story, I couldn't help but laugh and be mortified for her at the same time. Have kids, they said, such blessings.

My daughters were four years old and fifteen months old when my aunt passed away after a long battle with cancer. Her services were held three hours from where we lived and took place over two days. With two young children in tow, I decided to get a hotel and stay the night between the visita-

tion and funeral. At the time, my husband had a relatively new job and couldn't take time off work to attend with me. Thankfully, my mother lived nearby and offered to travel with my kids and me. Knowing that most of my large family would be present, I reached into the back of the girls' closet to find their beautifully made yet rarely worn lovely dresses and carefully packed them along with a fancy (read clean) pair of shoes for each of them. I conveniently forgot the fact that my four-year-old absolutely detested anything slightly restricting or uncomfortable.

The morning of the funeral was extremely hectic. My youngest doesn't sleep well away from home, therefore neither do I. Amidst getting the three of us ready, I also needed to pack all of our stuff and load the car since our checkout was during the funeral service. However, I made sure to leave enough time to apply my makeup and put in my seldom-used contacts. My aunt wished that all of her nieces would be the pallbearers at her funeral, which was an honor, but definitely put pressure on me to try and look nice. As a stay-at-home mom, my daily uniform consisted of old t-shirts made for easy nursing access, yoga pants worn thin in the thigh area, glasses, a messy bun, and Chapstick.

Honestly, I don't remember what was said at her funeral. All I can recall is the scathing stares of my extended relatives as I tried to (unsuccessfully) quietly unwrap the packaged activity I had stowed in the diaper bag. The multiple trips my four-

year-old needed to take to the bathroom and the subsequent banging of the double doors each time we exited and re-entered the sanctuary. I swear, there is something about a church that makes my children's bladders go into overdrive. They won't use the bathroom for six hours straight at home, and I have to threaten them to get them to sit on the toilet. When I was actually in the sanctuary and not in the bathroom, I was chasing my youngest back and forth down the side aisle of the church as she kept sprinting away; stopping every few steps to pick up and replace the shoes she was tossing behind her like turtle shells in Mario Kart.

I was perspiring, the sweat visibly dripping down my face, both from embarrassment and physical activity. It was when I tried wiping the offending droplets from my eyes that the day went downhill. In doing so, I accidentally knocked out one of my contacts. When I say "I'm blind without my glasses," I mean it. If my husband moves my shampoo in the shower, I will lather up with whatever is in its place that's around the same shape and color because I can't read what I'm using.

Not long after I lost fifty percent of my vision, the priest called for the pallbearers to come up. I had sat semi-isolated from as many people as I could in an effort not to be a nuisance, but by the time I was able to get my niece's attention to watch my girls, and able to make my way to the middle of the sanctuary, the casket was already half-way down the aisle and on its way out of the church. I jogged behind, trying to catch up while keeping one closed so I could see, ultimately looking like a sweaty version of popeye, the sailor man wobbling in heels like a baby giraffe. I exited the church just in time to see my cousins and sisters loading my dear, sweet aunt into the hearse. I did an about-face and made my way back into the church to collect my kids, and whatever was left of my dignity.

I learned a lot of valuable lessons that day. Here is my list of "should haves": I should have asked a family member to sit with us ahead of time; giving me someone to tag team with during the shoe chasing and bathroom trips and eliminating the need to frantically but discreetly find someone to sit with the girls when I needed to be a pallbearer. I should have packed far more entertainment for my little ones, unboxed and prepped ahead of time. I should have made sure my daughter with the borderline sensory disorder would wear the clothes I picked out for her before packing them. Her being miserable and complaining about tights and dress shoes that were 1/2 size too big was far worse than her showing up in leggings and some boots. Finally, I should have lowered my unfair expectations for both myself and my girls. I was trying too hard to "look the part" of a perfect stay-at-home mom in front of our family. I didn't consider that the three of us in our constraining dresses and unbearable shoes, trying to be "proper," was like putting lipstick on a pig. That just isn't who we are.

What should you take away from my story? Be yourself. Ask for help. Pack more quiet entertainment than you think you will need. Most importantly, don't chase the casket. Just sit quietly on the sidelines and relinquish your spot as a pall-bearer. Your aunt would understand; she was a mother of five.

-A story from my besties life-

To say I can relate is an understatement. "You're so lucky!" Those are the words I hear most often when I tell people that I am a stay-at-home mom. I would agree; I am very fortunate to be able to spend a copious amount of time with my kids. However, I'm not sure "lucky" is the best word to describe my job (yes, being a stay-at-home mom is definitely a job).

This type of child-rearing is hands-on, in-the-trenches, marathon pace mothering. It's rewarding but also incredibly exhausting. And not just physically exhausting, but also mentally taxing. I'm sure there are women out there who find stay-at-home parenting to be blissfully joyful. They probably look like the picture of perfection while cozied up on their spotless couch, in their expertly decorated living room, with their angelic children hanging on every word of the highly educational book they are reading. At least, I envision these types of mothers existing, and this perfection stereotype is one of the reasons why I find stay-at-home parenting to be so mentally arduous.

In reality, though, most of us are just trying to do our best raising our children, keeping up with the housework, and tackling family finances. This is a book for those women. The ones who are thankful and happy to be stay-at-home moms but aren't disillusioned about what the job description entails. Have you ever found yourself talking into your coffee cup instead of your phone because you are trying to do too many things at once? I'm willing to bet I'm not the only one. There I was, on a mini staycation, trying to give my kids some sort of a fun summer while trying to work and figure out the upcoming school schedules. I had my computer and pool towels in one hand and my coffee in the other while frantically searching for the room key and trying to carry on a conversation. I set down my phone instead of my coffee and didn't realize it until I was talking into a cup. I melted to the floor, laughing hysterically as I heard the person on the phone shout, "What? I can't hear you." I knew then that I needed to stop, breathe and simply enjoy the vacation. I had forgotten so quickly why I needed the break in the first place. Being a mother, wife, friend, daughter, and part-time employee is exhausting.

My husband and I live on a grain and livestock farm with three kids. My days are filled with dirt, poop (from multiple sources), mayhem, laughter, and love. I'm a preschool teacher, cheerleading coach, babysitter, friend, daughter, and writer in my spare time. Raising children is not an easy task. It is a constant struggle trying to maintain a balance between work life and family life. The feeling of being pulled in multiple directions is constant. One minute I'm planning projects for the preschool, the next, I'm running through a cornfield chasing loose cows while yelling at the kids not to move a muscle. There is never a dull moment. I have been a stay-at-home mom, a full-time working mom, and a part-time working mom; throughout all of them, I am always a "not enough" mom. In every situation, there is always the notion that there is not enough of me to go around.

After the birth of my first child, I decided that being a stay-at-home mom would be best for my family. After eight years of that, I decided that my children drive me crazy, so I worked full-time. Working full-time with kids was considerably different than when I was childless, so I went part-time. Part-time isn't what I expected either, but I'm hanging in there. Figuring out what works best for my family and me has been trial and error. I have done it all! If you are thinking about making the transition to being a stay-at-home mom, or if you find yourself suddenly thrown into stay-at-home motherhood, I have got your back—tips, guidelines, hilariously unfortunate stories; all things that will hopefully help you find your balance.

I have a bachelor's degree in psychology with a minor in child and family services and ten years of experience raising children. Do I have all the answers? Definitely not. But I have a few ideas, suggestions, and relatable tales that let you know you're not alone. I still walk into a room and forget why. I make lists and schedules and yet sometimes struggle with what I'm doing. I yell at the kids, I yell at the dog, I yell at the chickens, I yell just to make sure I'm still conscious. Then I cry because I yelled. I know my kids deserve grace and compassion even though I may have asked them nicely 783 times. I know it's not the dog's fault the chickens play mind games with her. And I know it's foolish to yell at ninja chickens who keep getting out, ruining my yard, and taunting my dog despite my best efforts. I cry because everything I do never seems to be enough in my mind. I may not have figured out how to shed the mom guilt, but I have learned that being able to laugh at yourself and show yourself kindness is quite helpful. Also, having a good hiding spot in your house where you can secretly eat your feelings now and again is pretty important too.

This book will hopefully guide you through the process of figuring out if staying at home is the right choice for you. Whether it was your own decision or you were tossed into it and are just trying to survive. There are so many things I wish someone would have warned me about before I started my journey; the good days and bad days, the push and pull between wanting to stay home with your kids and simultaneously wanting to run for the hills, the tricks on how to make life work with one income. Sure, the trials still would've happened, but maybe they wouldn't have knocked me down so hard. Even just knowing that I was not alone in my feelings and struggles would have been a welcomed understanding. As a veteran stay-at-home mother, I found the experience to be a mixed blessing, and this book will get honest about both the ups and downs of being a stay-at-home mom. Hopefully, we can learn from each other, support each other, and affirm one another's suspicions that stay-at-home mother-hood isn't easy or joyful all the time; and that's okay.

1

THE PROS AND CONS OF BEING A STAY-AT-HOME MOM

Is this actually happening? What on Earth made me start thinking about this? Transitioning to being a stay-at-home mom is a huge decision! Am I sure that I am ready for this? Can I really do this? Should I talk to someone about this? Why am I so stressed out already?

I'm not a betting gal, but I would wager that these are the questions running through your mind. This train of thought has probably been on repeat since you began thinking about being a stay-at-home mom. After all, it was my internal monologue too.

Ten years ago, I was in this exact frame of mind; nine months pregnant with my first child and completely terrified. My mind was about as overloaded as my poor swollen ankles. To say that my schedule was all over the place was an understatement. I bounced between three work shifts. I was spending my days as a 40-hour a week CNA and waitressing in the evenings. My husband had an equally taxing routine, working seven days a week and sometimes pulling 18 hour days. And, just to add a bit more craziness to the mix, we were devoted to our family farm. Growing grain and raising livestock is also a full-time job.

I would love to say that before we decided to start a family, we researched the changes it would bring to our lives, but that would be a complete lie. Blindsided by baby bliss, we didn't consider our hectic work schedules or the fact that we may need to adjust them to accommodate childcare. Like genuine new (*read naive*) parents, it wasn't until we got that glorious positive test that the reality sank in.

I knew that caring for a baby would be a full-time job too. My sweet and supportive partner was already working nearly every waking minute, and my routine was far from consistent. A quick hello here and a peck on the cheek there felt like all we had time for with how little our schedules overlapped. Now that I look back on it, how we even managed to get pregnant is a complete mystery.

I was thrilled that we were expecting, but I couldn't deny my anxiety. My first thoughts were, "Crap, how in the heck are we going to add a child to all this mayhem?" Then, "Who in their right mind decides having children is a good idea!" Thoughts of the future and questions of "how" plagued me at night. As I lay there, I wondered, "Do I need a live-in nanny? Are there babysitters that work all sorts of odd hours? How expensive are these people? Can babies ride on tractors? Is it weird if I waitress with a baby strapped to my back? Maybe I'll make better tips because my customers will feel bad for me."

On top of struggling with all the other worries first-time moms think about, I repeatedly went over every option to make our new reality work. It was impossible, partly because I had no clue what having a newborn was all about (in case my tractor question didn't clue you in). I honestly thought I would have a baby, and life would go back to normal. However, precisely what this new version of normal looked like and whether or not my husband and I could handle it with our hectic schedules was unclear. Secretly I wondered, did I want to "handle it," or did I want to experience it? Needless to say, I was in for a very rude awakening. As I would find out, normal and postpartum certainly don't go hand in hand.

After sleepless hours of pondering, I was mentally, physically, and emotionally exhausted. So one night, I did what I usually do when I'm trying to make a decision, grab a pen and paper and start writing a list. I wanted to lay it all out. What were our options when it came down to caring for a baby and working? Could we hire a nanny? Could we flex our schedules? Could I stay home and care for the baby myself? Thoughts, questions, expectations, and emotions swirled.

A list of pros and cons can go a long way when faced with a life-changing decision. It is a simple tool that can give a clear picture of the positives and negatives associated with your decision. As you do your research, gather arguments, and build your list, new perspectives, ideas, and even gaps in your thinking will present themselves.

Making such a huge decision about whether or not our finances, our relationship, and our family could survive the transition called for a thorough review of the facts. With a pros and cons list, you can weigh your arguments against one another. Putting your thoughts on paper in a simple this-versus-that list can make it easier to remove emotion from the equation and aid you in taking an unbiased look at some truths.

I think I stayed awake for three hours that night just making my list. As new thoughts led to possible problems and also creative solutions, I jotted them down. I happily penned away my pros and cons list, acting as both a fantastic stress reliever and preventative measure against wetting the bed. With a baby kicking my bladder every five minutes, I had a real fear of soaking the sheets if I was unconscious.

I urge you not to make your pros and cons list in your head arbitrarily. It will blow up, trust me. While it may seem like an effortless task, so many thoughts and emotions go into building a pros and cons list that you can quickly become overwhelmed. Here is how I like to begin. I start by dividing my paper into two columns. Then, I write all my pros on one side and my cons on the other side. At first, I will write as fast as I can. But, seriously, don't think, just write, letting the jumble of what-ifs and anxieties spill out onto the paper. No thought or idea is too insignificant to earn a place on the list. Then, when you have your list, take a look at how your pros and cons balance out. You can likely counter some of the cons with some of the pros. But undoubtedly, you may end up with a few outliers. So focus on the cons now. Can any of these cons be turned into a pro with some creative thinking and a unique solution?

One of my most significant and most pressing cons when becoming a stay-at-home mom was "loss of income." Thinking of no longer having my portion of earnings coming in was a lot to grapple with. I liked the lifestyle that two paychecks afforded us, and I appreciated that it paid the bills even more. As I pondered on this con, I had an epiphany. Becoming a stay-at-home mom would take one of our most significant bills off the table. Did you know that parents with children under age five living in the US spend around $42 billion annually for early childcare[1]? We were looking at paying what I felt like was an excessive amount if we wanted to enroll our baby in daycare. Staying at home with our little one meant that the "loss of income," which is a huge con, could be adapted to a "no child care expense," which is a significant pro. Moving on down the list, I found that my con of "no adult time" could be turned into the pro of "spending more time with other mom friends on playdates" (which may or may not have turned out to be true...). But I was optimistic! I'm not always a glass half full type of gal, but I learned that when you want something bad enough, you will find a way to make it work.

Prioritizing your pros and cons list is a big part of solving the stay-at-home problem. Find what you are willing to give up and what makes the sacrifice worth it. For me, the deciding factor was being able to experience my children's lives every day. It was the most deserving of our sacrifices and ended up being the most worthwhile cause on my list. Thinking of dropping our kids off for hours at a daycare center then picking them up only to take them home to make dinner, blow through a whirlwind nighttime routine, and then put them to bed was a gut-punch. I did not want to be there only for a few minutes in the car and maybe a couple of hours at night. I also did not want to struggle to find family time on the weekends between chores and activities. I wanted to be there day in and day out. Whatever your driving factor, you will find that it shapes and prioritizes your list. Our lists will likely look very different, but here is an example of a few ideas you may want to add to your pros and cons list.

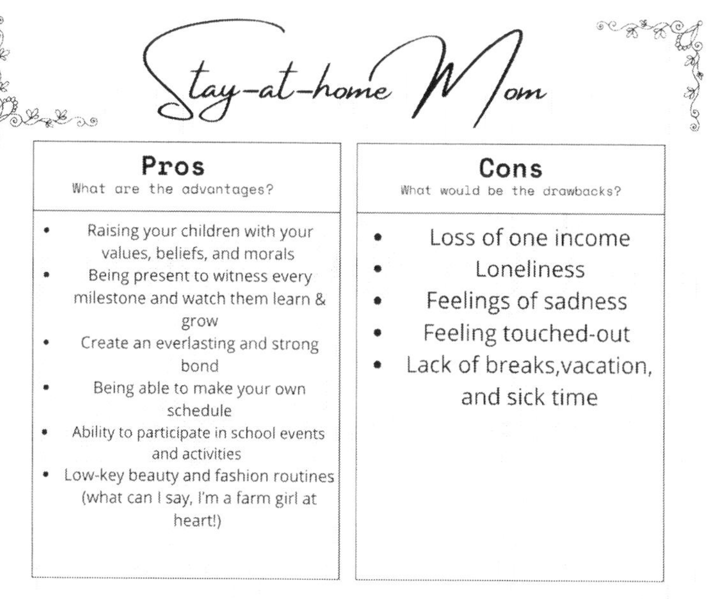
Stay-at-home Mom

Pros What are the advantages?	Cons What would be the drawbacks?
• Raising your children with your values, beliefs, and morals • Being present to witness every milestone and watch them learn & grow • Create an everlasting and strong bond • Being able to make your own schedule • Ability to participate in school events and activities • Low-key beauty and fashion routines (what can I say, I'm a farm girl at heart!)	• Loss of one income • Loneliness • Feelings of sadness • Feeling touched-out • Lack of breaks,vacation, and sick time

By the end, I felt better. Assured? No. Decided? Certainly not. But clearer? Yes. I was beginning to see a path to tackling this decision and coming up with a solution that would make sense for our family. So my advice to you is to make a list. Grab a mug of tea or glass of wine, your favorite cozy blanket, go to your ideal thinking spot, and relax. Close your eyes and clear your mind as much as possible, put on your favorite playlist, and breathe. I won't lie to you; it can be daunting, but it is doable. Getting over this first hurdle will lay a strong foundation for your argument to transition to stay-at-home motherhood. Let's take a deeper dive into some topics your list should include, specifically finances, emotions, and relationships.

FINANCES FIRST

I never really had a budget or even a clue about the money coming in and going out. Every bill I had was set up for autopay, and I trusted the bank to let me know when I didn't have any money left. Terrible practices, I know. But, I was young and didn't have to worry about paying for things because my husband and I both made decent money. That and the fact that when you are sans children, you can choose to spend money on almost whatever you want.

I may not have had a solid grasp of the numbers. Still, I was pretty positive that dropping one income and introducing another dependent human being into the equation would lead to drastic lifestyle changes. The bank would be contacting me for sure. Unfortunately, the new expenses became exceedingly accurate when I began to procure quotes for full-time childcare -- ouch.

Despite my lackluster finance skills, I began to make a budget. Correction, I Googled how to make a budget. I was no accounting wizard, but if I was going to be the CFO of our family, I needed help. Google was my BFF. Which led me to my favorite finance teacher, the one and only, Dave Ramsey.

I followed his wise words, "A budget is telling your money where to go instead of wondering where it went," and set down to scratch out where every penny was going. Not only monthly bills and habitual stops by the local coffee shop, but also unforeseen circumstances.

Say your partner suddenly is unable to work, an illness that comes out of nowhere, or an ultrasound that reveals two heartbeats instead of one. Make sure you have all your finances in order and can realistically survive without your income. I'm talking about calculating every cost, planned, unplanned, typical, atypical, monthly, biannually, and yearly. It's a big undertaking. Simply thinking about writing out a budget of this caliber was enough to give me anxiety, pen hovering above the paper. But thinking about taking such a giant leap without knowing and securing that we could survive financially spurred me into action.

If you are drowning in debt, this may not be the best time to give up your income. If you can, great; if not, start thinking of ways to supplement your income. Odd jobs, working from home, organ donorship, just kidding, don't go that far. I mean, the thought did cross my mind, along with exotic dancing, but ultimately my fallback was waitressing the odd shift when necessary. Whatever you are comfortable with, research it and see if it's a viable option.

INSURANCE PREMIUMS AND PEANUT SHELLS

Along with finances comes the topic of insurance. Do you carry the benefits? What will happen if you decide to transition to being a stay-at-home mom? How will your family be covered? Will additional policies need to be taken out? Does it fit into your fabulous new budget?

Insurance should not be an afterthought. While your budget may include the occasional sick visit or check-up, medical emergencies can wreak havoc on well-laid financial plans. For example, what if your child decides to eat a fist full of peanut shells and, as a result, chokes? Would you be able to call an ambulance without going into severe debt? What if said child develops a wheeze after this incident and needs to see a specialist? Then needs to have a procedure to make sure his lungs are free of peanut shells. Next, he ends up back at the children's hospital an hour away with more complications that turn out to be a coincidental virus. Yes, that happened, and it was a nightmare, mentally and financially. Will this oversight, which will ultimately haunt you for the rest of your life, cause extreme financial hardship, or do you have decent insurance?

Oh, the joys of being a responsible adult. Maybe these what-ifs are just the musings of a slightly paranoid, definitely sleep-deprived, first-time mom, but they ran through my head. As I was about to enter this new chapter of adulthood, I could see why adults tell children to be a kid for as long as possible. Adulting is not as much fun as being a kid; somehow, eating ice cream for dinner doesn't make up for having a reasonable budget.

EVERY MOM IS A WORKING MOTHER

As I pondered all the medical mishaps my unborn child could encounter, I began to think about the emotional aspects of transitioning to a stay-at-home mom.

Mothers in the workforce have the stability of an income and possibly insurance with benefits. Yet, no matter the circumstance, moms who work outside the home and stay-at-home moms still suffer from dreaded mom guilt. Full-time working moms suffer just as much, if not more, than stay-at-home moms. It starts when they're an infant, and the hazy but sweet days of maternity leave come to an end. Suddenly, the desire of wanting just a single minute alone is replaced with apprehension. Then, there is the constant fear of missing important milestones, like first words or first steps. It doesn't get any easier as your children grow and have practices, recitals, and games to attend. The feeling of not spending enough time with your children is pervasive. Will you miss having treasured adventures with them? Reading books on the couch or simply picking them up from school? Just thinking about sending them to daycare was enough to cause a pit in my stomach.

Sadly, the choice to become a stay-at-home mom isn't even on the table for many mothers. They have to work because it is hands-down the best choice for their family. On the contrary, there are plenty of moms who enjoy working outside of the home. They like having a profession and thrive in their careers. They don't mind sending their child to daycare because trained care-givers are just as good at teaching their little ones and can probably do it with more patience. While the idea of being a stay-at-home mom may occasionally cross their minds, it tends to be fleeting as they are perfectly content balancing their career and children. But even these women are not immune to mom guilt. The guilt they may feel is because they are happy and feel guilty for being happy! Feeling guilty for being a happy working mom... Isn't it crazy? It's just one of the many characteristics of motherhood. Unfortunately, this characteristic may be society-induced. Social norms may lull them into thinking that they should not feel so happy with their choice to work outside of the home. Instead, they should be at home, simultaneously nursing, teaching their infant another language, and cooking gourmet meals while keeping their house immaculate. I mean, seriously, some people believe this is what motherhood is!

Unfortunately, even June Cleaver probably wasn't a stranger to mom guilt. Stay at home moms question if they're doing the best thing for their kids. Should they be sending them to preschool to socialize and learn? Are they doing enough? And not just enough for their kids, but what about their career and their home? Their social life and physical health? You can do the laundry, sweep, wipe snotty noses, cook dinner, go on a walk, and still feel the guilt creeping in. Maybe it's because you think that you should have a "real" job. Or, you feel like you didn't spend enough time practicing reading with your kid. The list goes on. The idea that we women should have it all is frankly a lie. But, nevertheless, knowing it is a falsehood doesn't stop the guilt.

I have mom friends in various stages of motherhood and experiencing a diverse range of situations, and guess what? They each struggle with their own mom guilt in some form or another. In addition to mom guilt, being a stay-at-home mom comes with a particular set of physical and emotional challenges.

In some aspects, it may be more challenging than working outside of the home. I don't want to burst your bubble of mornings spent frolicking in the sun with your child and afternoons with them happily snoozing while you take care of some housework, but what you think being a stay-at-mom looks like is probably far from reality. It is hard. Some days you will be bone-tired. Lack of break times and paid vacations, and even weekends will do that to you. But it is also emotionally challenging. During my recent poll of stay-at-home moms on my Facebook page, almost all of them complain of depression and feelings of sadness and isolation. I'm not implying that your children will make you depressed, but mommin' ain't easy, and anyone who tells you otherwise probably hasn't been a stay-at-home mom.

Working moms commonly have an escape or an out, even if it isn't what most of us would consider a getaway. They can go home to escape the stress of their job or go to work to escape the pressures at home. Either way, they have somewhere to *go*. Honestly, those mothers who work full-time from home are the real VIPs. If you know someone who works remotely from their house full of small children, hug them, send them wine, and tell them how amazing they are. Unfortunately, stay-at-home moms do not have the luxury of escape. Their home is their work, the place they are supposed to retreat to, and sometimes it can feel as if the walls are closing in.

For me, constantly having a child or children around who track my every move and proceed to cry the second I leave the room makes it pretty hard to escape. They crave interaction and thrive on my undivided attention. It is entirely natural and developmentally appropriate. But oh, how I wish they understood the need for a couple of minutes to collect myself. Or the fact that most people have privacy while they are pooping, not a tiny person handing you toilet paper asking if you need help wiping. I mean, it's a nice gesture but not necessary, little dude. My lack of coworkers makes it tough to vent to another adult. Even a call seems impossible. If it isn't the screaming, it's the million and one interruptions that make conversation attempts far from worthwhile. Phone calls have become my luxury, day late texts my default, and you can forget about meeting up with a friend in person.

The sheer amount of stuff that needs to be packed, organized, and carried makes it look like I am a sherpa leading a month-long expedition. The amount of frustration I get from walking-age children, who frequently suffer the sudden and mysterious illness that hinders their ability to move, is not worth trying to go anywhere. I love my girlfriends, but in all honesty, just the thought of loading my car and my kids stress me out. Then, having to watch them like a hawk, running interference, operating a mobile snack stand, and trying to enjoy a conversation is enough to make me want to stay home indefinitely. It so clearly illustrates the feeling of no escape. Days bleed into one another, each one bringing the same routine. There is no respite, hence the depression and sadness. Feelings of being alone. Feelings of being a failure because every stupid craft you try on Pinterest never turns out like the polished image framed by beaming kids and their perfect mom. Whenever you try to shower and shave to feel human again, something happens, and you end up running out of the shower. Hair full of shampoo, one leg shaved, the other looking like a Goldendoodle, all because your toddler's show turned off on the television. Finally, once you've calmed your child and your heart rate, you decide you're clean enough and rinse your hair in the kitchen sink over the dirty dishes. Hey, any type of soap can only help the crusty mess, right? As you gaze out over the kitchen sink, into your yard strewn with toys, you resolve to take a break—just a few short minutes to yourself. So, you slip back into your recently cleaned and organized room only to discover it is now a mess and covered in crap. Literal crap because the kid learned how to paint with the contents of his diaper. The same kid who can't figure out how to eat a puff is now freaking Van Gough. Helplessness sets in, and you can feel the emotional tidal wave surging. The tears that began with your heightened emotional and hormonal state during pregnancy are the new normal.

All those stories of mothers running away and starting a new life? I get it. I will admit that the thought has ever so briefly crossed my mind. However, the idea is quickly overpowered because I love these little turds and can't imagine life without them. Never could I walk out on my children. They are my world, but I am not ashamed to say that motherhood is damn hard. The mental duress coupled with the physical weariness is enough to send you down a dark road.

It isn't my desire to frighten you away from being a stay-at-home or use fear tactics to scare you into changing your mind. I only wish to paint a realistic picture of what some days will look like. There are days when everything falls perfectly into place, and then there are days when it all comes crashing down around you.

Understanding that being a stay-at-home mom will probably look very different than how you envisioned is part of the transition.

Before you leap wholeheartedly into staying home with your children, make sure you have a safety net. Do you have a support system? Do you have people that will come and help you clean or watch the kid so you can sleep? Do you have a partner in crime? Are they on board? All of these questions are hopefully enough to make anyone stop and think. But, I mean really, think about this decision. It's not all rainbows and butterflies as social media would have us believe. Most mothers know it will be challenging, but thinking about it and living it are two very different things.

Take a look back at your pros and cons list. I encourage you to jot down a few thoughts about how transitioning to a stay-at-home mom will affect your mental health and possibly even your physical health. It won't hurt to include ideas about how your new role may affect those closest to you as well, particularly your partner and your children.

GETTING OUR HANDS DIRTY

The seeds have now been sown, the idea of becoming a stay-at-home mom has been planted. Now, it is time to get our hands dirty and put in the work. To see your dream come to fruition, we need to take some time to cultivate it. So let us start diving deep into the topics we have just discussed, wading through the what-ifs, and finally making a plan for a successful transition. Along the way, I'll share a few of my real-life experiences that may give you a few tips about how to make this stay-at-home-mom thing work or at least give you a good laugh.

I'll admit, my house isn't spotless, and my kids aren't learning multiple languages while I prepare a four-course meal. But I do think I have come a long way from that mom crying in her poop-covered bedroom. I have since gained valuable insight. I wish someone had shared the wisdom with young Andie when she was setting off on the most incredible journey of her life - motherhood.

2

FINANCES: PLANNING TO HAVE A PLAN

Did the pros on your list win out? Are you invested in becoming a stay-at-home mom and making it work? The first, and in my opinion, most important thing is to get your finances in order. The simplest solution to do this? Make a budget!

Okay, so simple probably isn't the right word to describe budgeting. However, planning for your expenses and knowing where every penny is going is the *best* solution to getting your finances in order.

Before becoming a one-income household, we didn't have a budget (crazy, right?). I was blissfully unaware of how much we were earning and where that money was going. Thanks to an autopay system offered by our bank, the bills were being paid. We also felt comfortable enough to spend some here and there on eating out, clothes, and the occasional vacation. Like millions of other Americans, we worked to make ends meet and just carried on as usual.

While I may have been living in a state of peaceful naivete, if I stopped to think about our financial state and spending habits, I became a bit freaked out. I didn't need to do an in-depth analysis of my budgeting skills to know that, in short, they sucked. But as much as I loathe financial planning, the realization that subtracting one income while adding a family member could tip the scales in the wrong direction spurred me into action. I had to get things in order and fast! I started by making a budget. But, who am I kidding? I had no clue how to accomplish that! So I began scouring the internet. I am about to share some helpful tips with you that will save you hours of research and protect you from the infinite rabbit holes you could get lost in for days. There are indeed plenty of budgeting apps out there, but you can do it on your own too! Online spreadsheets are handy, or you can scratch one out with a pen and paper if you prefer. Understanding how to make a bare-bones budget without using a digital tool will empower you with the knowledge of how you can afford to be a stay-at-home mom.

You can't spend what you don't have. So start by listing the income you will have and the frequency in which you'll receive it. In other words, does your partner get paid weekly? Bi-weekly? Monthly? Now, don't lose hope just yet. I was a tad scared when faced with the numbers of how much one income is. Living on only my husband's paycheck didn't initially seem within the realm of reason. But knowing where your family stands financially is just the first step.

Next, make a list of all your debts. Every single debt. Credit cards, medical bills, car loans, even student loans if you have them. Adulting is fun, isn't it? Alright, once you have your list, put your debts in order from least to the greatest amount owed. Large debts likely have a lot of interest, but that considerable amount owed can be a bear to tackle mentally and financially. A tactic I love from one of my favorite financial gurus is to pay off the smallest debt first and gradually work your way up to the largest debt. Each time you pay off a smaller debt, you gain a few things. First, additional income, not to add to your pocket, but to put towards the next debt on your list. Secondly, you gain confidence and motivation; one debt down, only a few more to go! My husband and I find that the small wins we achieve by paying off little debts are enough to keep us working hard towards our goal of being entirely debt-free. If you have the opportunity to pay off your debts this way, I highly recommend it. Though whatever you do, avoid being sent to collections for a delinquent minimum payment.

Debt is just one side of the coin when it comes to expenses. You will also have a steady stream of routine bills and somewhat regular expenditures. It can be helpful to look at recurring bills first because these are everyday necessities required to survive. Paying whatever bills are necessary to keep your home, whether rent or mortgage, is essential. Then, you have your general costs of living. These include things like phone bills, electricity, water, etc. Finally, don't forget about fees that are due quarterly, biannually, or yearly. Trash disposal, insurance, auto registration, all of these expenses should be factored into your monthly budget even though they don't occur each month. Is your head spinning yet? I'm getting sweaty just thinking about when I began my budgeting journey.

Try to limit this section of your budget to basic survival expenses. These bills usually don't change too much from month to month, which helps designate what your income needs to go towards. Next, list expenses that are important to your survival but can fluctuate. These include grocery bills, clothing, and fuel costs. While you need these things to maintain a standard of living, you can typically pare down what you buy or rideshare with a friend, cutting your costs.

I like to organize my expenses into a few different tabs on my spreadsheet. One tab is for monthly bills, another is for non-monthly bills, and a third tab is a running total of all my bills combined. This helps me to budget appropriately not only for each month but also for the entire year. When you are just starting with your budget, you may not have a solid grasp of your yearly expenses. But I promise that you will get better as you go along. For example, I have tracked our family's annual costs for a couple of years now and have gradually learned about how much we spend, on average, on significant expenses. For example, our farm has a propane tank. It only gets filled once it is down to a quarter of a tank. We can only estimate when that will be based on our use, the weather, and other factors. But let me tell you when that bill comes due, it is considerable; and due all at once. Instead of allowing it to make a massive dent in our monthly income, we prepare ahead of time by averaging how much we spend each year on refills and dividing that by twelve. This number is how much we need to set aside each month to cover our propane bill when the well, or tank, runs dry. Another example would be property taxes. Our property taxes are not escrowed, so they need to be paid twice a year. We diligently dole out this money into a separate account every month to be prepared for tax season.

We have learned through painful trial and error that setting aside monthly money for large, semi-regular bills is by far better than draining our accounts. In the past, we were in a pinch due to several of our substantial bills coming due at once. Property taxes, bi-annual car insurance, and propane. It was a doozy. Thankfully we had extra income from the farm that season or I am not sure how we would have paid them. It's a scary place to be in, especially when you rely only on one income and don't have a steady avenue for earning extra money. This is why saving monthly for significant non-monthly expenses is crucial for financial success.

After you have spent some time listing your must-pay expenses and their respective amounts, it's time to figure out where the rest of your money is going. Now isn't the time to be coy. You need to write down where, when, and how you honestly spend your money. Do you have a Target habit? Does your family like to eat out regularly? Did that once-a-month splurge on Starbucks somehow morph into a daily coffee run? Please don't lie to yourself because it will only end up hurting you in the long run. If you know you regularly spend money on any number of lifestyle choices; clothing, dining out, fixing up old automobiles, then write it down and try to come up with an approximation of how much you spend each month.

Oomph. Let me tell you, my list was not pretty. I was terrified of the possibility that when I did the calculations, I would find we had been living in the red. But let me put some of your fears aside. These expenses are not do or die. You can survive without them. They are purely lifestyle choices that can be cut back on and adjusted. When you look at them in this light, you find that they are opportunities to prove you can survive on one income, and you will do whatever it takes to make staying home with your child a reality.

Now it's time to crunch some numbers. How does your spreadsheet balance out? Are you earning more than you're spending or vice versa? Chances are, when you go from two incomes to one, you will need to refigure your calculations as your spending will probably outpace your income. So, find what you can live without. I thought that there was no way I could live without cable. I need my guilty-pleasure reality show once a week, and I like to enjoy a cup of coffee with the local news now and again. But it turns out that cutting the cord was pretty easy, as was letting go of a few other lifestyle must-haves that weren't must-haves at all. I canceled every monthly subscription that I had signed up for. I was a bit shocked to find out how many had slowly accumulated over the years; look at all the money we could have been saving! I then moved onto, trying to lower our bills and debts. I called each and every single company I owed money to, and I haggled. I was able to talk down our phone bill, our electricity, and many others. When I was finished, I was only paying for our necessities and paying the bare minimum rate. Now that I have three kids, I don't have extra free time for watching television or participating in monthly subscription boxes anyway, and I greatly appreciate how much we save by canceling all of these "extras."

There are many other ways to save money when on a budget that don't involve lowering rates on your necessities—quite the opposite in fact. The main habit to change is scaling down your indulgences. One of the biggest budget offenders is going out to eat. If you were to add up all your dining out receipts, I bet you would be shocked, as many families usually spend the most money on this indulgence. I was often guilty of falling into the trap of just running through a drive-through or hitting up a restaurant because I didn't have the time or energy to cook. Less mess and no prep? Mama's here for it! Until I realized just how much that was eating into our earnings. I started meal planning to combat my unpreparedness and hectic schedule. I made an inventory of everything in our fridge, freezer, and pantry, then came up with dinners using things we already had on hand! Not only did this decrease the number of times we dined out, but it also cut our grocery bill in half and helped me reduce our food waste. I became a stickler for only buying what is on my grocery list and using up food at home before it could go bad and had to be tossed out. With a plan in hand and organized pantries at the ready, I tackled lunches and snacks too. I have meals, snacks, and drinks packed and ready to go if we're leaving the house. Playdates, the zoo, a trip to the doctor's office? You can bet I have food stored away like a squirrel in winter just waiting for the "I'm hungry!" cries of my young from the backseat. This new habit makes it so much easier to drive past the drive-through line.

Food is only a piece of the pie. Clothing, accessories, fancy toiletries, and more are slicing into your budget. My advice? Use what you have. Don't be persuaded by that latest hand soap scent, new color of eyeshadow, or trendy t-shirt that you likely already have buried in your closet. Brands are masters at fooling us into thinking we need the latest and greatest to meet the status quo. I'm not saying you have to adopt the mom bun, loose tee, and holey jeans (which are totally in vogue right now), but you probably don't need a wardrobe update every month or even every year. For my kids that are growing like weeds, I frequently shop secondhand. There are some great items at salvation armies, social media mom-to-mom groups, and online community garage sale websites. I regularly find brand-new or barely used items for a couple of bucks. If I can't find it online or in goodwill (which is rare), I ask friends and relatives for their hand-me-downs. I can probably count on one hand the times I have had to buy clothes for my children because all my family members know that I'll happily take what they no longer need. Many of them are delighted at the prospect of not having to go through items and try to sort them for sale or donation because they can simply box them up and leave them on their doorstep. I even offer to pick them up! I've come a long way from the girl who was too embarrassed to shop cheap or ask for no-longer-needed items. I am addicted to saving money now, especially if it affords me the lifestyle I want, staying home with my kiddos. I'm resourceful, having learned to make my laundry soap, I'm relentless in the fact that I *will* do whatever it takes to make this work for our family, and I'm rewarded with the opportunity to watch my children grow and learn every day.

Once you've cut, canceled, and slashed rates, you can calculate your total expenses for each month. This number is how much you absolutely need to pay the bills and basic necessities. It is non-negotiable. While I would love to congratulate you, we're not quite done yet! Your budget is now in place, but you still need to plan for those pesky unforeseen circumstances in life. When choosing to give up your second income, thinking of all the things that could go wrong and preparing for them becomes less of an exercise in pessimism and more of a plan that could save your family's livelihood. What if your partner fell ill or became injured and was unable to work? Does their job offer sick leave or disability pay? Can you expect disability coverage of 100% of their income, or is it less than their standard pay? If you can't count on your partner's employer to pay in full should illness or injury occur, then you need an emergency savings account.

Many people have a savings account; some regularly contribute while others haphazardly put in a few dollars here and there. Unfortunately, not everyone has an emergency savings account. In general, an emergency savings account should cover three to six months of your living expenses; or, that number we just calculated for bills, debts, and necessities. An account of this type is just for emergencies. This money should not be dipped into regularly, used to pay for vacations, or even to cover big-ticket items that aren't an emergency. It is your safety net, funds you can rely upon should something go wrong. This account should be started after you are out of debt, everything paid besides the mortgage. Once you have all of your debts paid off, it will be effortless to save for that emergency fund, along with doubling your mortgage payment.

If making regular payments to debts or just meeting your living expenses is difficult, you may need to search for ways to supplement your income. Thankfully, there are various ways that stay-at-home moms can earn extra money with a side hustle or a part-time job. I have a good friend who is a waitress on nights and weekends when her husband is available to be home with the kids. If you can (or want) to take on a flexible job with your schedule, go for it! This is perhaps the easiest way to make regular earnings to supplement your partner's paycheck.

But I understand how that isn't doable for some, whether it doesn't work for your schedule or you honestly don't want to commit to a job where someone else dictates where you need to be and when. Waitressing was something I did pre-stay-at-home-mom, and I could certainly do it again if it weren't for my husband's relentless work responsibilities. I'm grateful for his job and his work ethic, truly, but that leaves me with few options for how to make extra money. I narrowed it down to being a sales solicitor or a writer and seeing as I haven't found the time to complete a phone call in the past two years, my chances of being successful are pretty slim. So I opted for writing, a passion, and a possible supplement to our income. I have another friend who makes crafts in her spare time and sells them on Facebook, Etsy, and local craft fairs. Social media can prove itself beneficial for once by allowing you to reach out to local community members. You can quickly gauge what they need help with or any interest in products or services that you may be able to assist with. If you have a talent or a skill, share it with the world, and if you can make some money while doing it, that's a bonus.

If you find a way to earn a little bit of additional money, that's great! If not, you need to be extra conscious of your spending each month. While it is nice to have a budget in place, trying to keep track of all of these amounts and figures when you are preoccupied with caring for tiny humans is no easy task. Instead of trying to recall how much I have to spend on groceries as one child tries to squirm out of the shopping cart and the other is wrapped around my leg desperately begging for Oreos, my family relies on a more straightforward method. The envelope method. It has been popularized by quite a few financial wizards and programs, and we have found that it works pretty well for our family. To use this method, you need to have a series of envelopes. You can have physical envelopes, though this will require you to pay for almost everything with cash, or you can have virtual envelopes (read: accounts) with your bank. When a paycheck comes in, it isn't left to sit in your checking account.

Leaving it in checking can make it challenging to know how much you are spending on each budget line, and it can be tricky to see if you are indeed staying within budget each month. So, you will "pay" your envelopes with your paycheck to set aside exactly the amount of funds you have allocated for each category. For example, do you only have $500 set aside for food this month? Then the food envelope only gets $500. That is all you have to spend, no ifs, ands, or buts about it. I highly suggest paying your most essential envelopes first, like bills, food, and fuel to get to work. Another benefit of the envelope system is that it can keep you from overspending on lifestyle habits that you don't need. When you are finished contributing to all your necessities and still have money left, you can choose to put some in the dining out envelope or the entertainment envelope. If you don't have anything to spare, eating at a restaurant or going to a movie isn't a choice this month. It is a very black and white way to know where every penny is going so you can stick to your budget. If you immediately direct your paycheck into the correct envelope and only use what is in that envelope, overspending is nearly impossible.

Budgeting, even with all of your hard work and planning, is a balancing act. Fuel costs fluctuate, food prices vary, your children may get sick and need a doctor more one season than the next. But the point of a budget is to prepare as much as possible and plan for how your family can not just survive but thrive on one income without incurring any additional debt. I have often heard how lucky I am to be able to stay at home with my children. But, if you've just followed along and created a budget, then you know luck has nothing to do with it. It takes sacrifice, paring down our expenses, going without, and finding creative ways to supplement our income for many of us. But I believe that when I look back on the years when my children were young and knew I was there by their side day in and day out, it will all be worth it! I hope. I will leave you with an example of a monthly budget sheet.

MONTH OF:

INCOME

Date	Source	Amount

DEBT

Date	Deposit	Paid Date	Balance

SAVINGS

Date	Deposit	Paid Date	Balance

MONTHLY

Total Income	
Total Budget	
Total Savings	
Total Expenses	

BILL

Bill	Amount	Due Date	Paid Date

Notes

3

THE GRASS IS ALWAYS GREENER - TRANSITIONING WITH YOUR PARTNERS FULL SUPPORT

Having the support of your partner is pretty simple when neither of you has any expectations, frame of reference, or ideal image of what being a stay-at-home parent will look like. When I made the transition, we didn't personally know anyone who stayed home with their kids. We didn't have any friends, neighbors, or family to ask what it was honestly like. I had several mom friends, but their situations varied and weren't identical to what we were preparing to do. Some worked full time and relied on daycare, and others had family members who watched their children while they were at the office. I even knew a few parents who were able to bring their children to work with them. Every situation came with positives and negatives, which I learned from our regular get-togethers. It didn't seem like anyone's scenario was better than the others. Every family did what worked best for them, yet no one could escape the stress or worry. Anxiety about their children being at daycare for far too long. Worried about their kids not socializing early enough while being home with grandma, no one was immune. But you know what they say, the grass is always greener on the other side.

I can say that I thought, without a doubt, that the lawn of a stay-at-home moms' house was weeded, fertilized, edged, and fully prepped for a PGA tour. It was looking pretty good from where I stood, in a tangled mess of hectic schedules, mounting daycare costs, and mom-guilt that clawed at my legs like brambles. I was ready to give up my weedy mess and leap on over to the well-manicured pasture of the Joneses. My husband agreed and was fully supportive in the beginning. But instead of jumping in feet first, we tiptoed into the situation. After we had our first child, I didn't return to my job as a CNA. Caring for a little one, nursing 24/7, and running on a few precious hours of sleep left me exhausted. Exhaustion, coupled with my shifts being too inconsistent to find reliable childcare, made the decision to cut back on my career relatively easy. I started working part-time in a doctor's office and found a great caregiver for our child. Soon, we were expecting our second child. I think the miracle of birth is that all your memories of pregnancy and childbirth are somehow erased. If anyone recalled what the third trimester and labor were actually like, they would not be so eager to give their little one a sibling. But as I approached my due date, the miracle of my erased memories began to wear off. I recalled the exhaustion, the juggling of schedules, and the panic I faced when my caregiver couldn't make it or my child was sick and couldn't go to daycare. Speaking of childcare, what was the going rate for two kids, I wondered?

With baby number two ready to join us earth side any day now, we had some serious decisions to make, so we sat down and crunched some numbers. The decision became apparent very quickly. My take-home pay from the doctor's office was barely enough to cover daycare costs for two children. I would be working solely to send my kids to childcare. Together, we decided that it didn't make sense to continue sending our little ones to school. Unfortunately, neither of us had a family that could watch our children for free or at a discounted rate. The only solution was for me to stay home full time to raise our kids. We made a budget that suited our new, adjusted income and naively (*so naively*) thought, how hard could it be?

Pretty hard. The situation quickly began to wear on both my husband and me, mentally, physically, and emotionally. My garden of Eden that I had enviously once peeked at from my lawn turned out to be a fake astroturf that hid and covered a multitude of rough spots and difficulties. Most days, the grass was not greener on the other side. There were good days, there were bad days, and there were terrible days. For a while, it seemed as if the bad days were outweighing the good. With the arrival of our third child, the bad days seem to overtake the good days wholly. My nights were restless, my days were sleepless, and one exceptionally rough twenty-four hours ran into the next. My poor husband was crabby and apprehensive every time he came home. I can't blame him because I was irritable and edgy for him to come home. The opening of our garage door sent me running, not into his arms, but into our bedroom, door locked, just to find thirty minutes of peace. Unfortunately, after working a long shift, my husband wanted that same respite. He couldn't understand why I needed a moment's rest. Certainly not with both me and the house looking a mess. Once, he asked, "how sitting on the couch all day could be so hard." To say I was mad was an understatement. It took everything I had in me not to perform a full-speed running aerial kick to his face. I counted to ten and tried to collect myself, explaining why I was so exhausted. I never could fully detail what I did all day. I knew it was a lot. My weary mind and weakened body showed it was a lot; it was too much to recall fully. Mentally I was done. Exhaustion is a funny thing. You would think that it would make you unable to get out of bed, so tired that your arms and legs fail to obey your body. But oh no, my mom-bod carried on while my mind was asleep upstairs. I constantly fought to remember what I was doing, aimlessly walking into rooms (or walls) and wondering what I was doing there. When the kids took a nap or went down to bed, I was doing laundry, picking up toys, and trying to get ahead of the neverending dishes. To my husband, who wasn't a witness to all my hard work, it appeared as if I never made a dent in any chores. I just kept going on autopilot, day after day. I would break down in tears, and he would simply walk away. It was a very stressful time.

We didn't understand each other's roles anymore. While I may not have hated him, it sure felt like I did. I resented all of the things he was able to do. To me, he got a break all day long. He got to go to a gas station and actually go inside, maybe even purchase a snack solely for himself! He could go out to lunch with his coworkers. He could have uninterrupted conversations with adults. The list went on and on. As I picked clumps of playdough out of the carpet for the tenth time that day, I took inventory of all the things he could do that I couldn't. I was home cooking, cleaning, and taking care of the children. Each is an impossible task in itself. My kids were never pleased. The chores never finished. I was barely surviving each day while he got to live kid-free without a care in the world. But while I was tallying up my husband's offenses against me and our household, I failed to realize that maybe he resented me too. In his eyes, I was able to stay home all day. I didn't have to leave the house if I didn't want to. Heck, I didn't even have to get out of my pajamas! I was *able* to raise our kids. I got to be a part of their lives for more than just an hour after work before they went to bed. I was the parent they turned to when they needed someone to soothe their fears or cuddle them after a fall at the playground. I got to witness the milestones and the "firsts." I had a special bond with our children that he believed he could never have, working outside the home for most of the day, five days a week. I didn't have deadlines and due dates, people telling me where I had to be and when (if you don't count a demanding two-year-old). He resented me and my life of privileges and freedom. This resentment seeped into other areas of our life.

My husband knew from the start that my resignation would mean that he had to pick up the slack financially. But knowing and feeling are two different things. He would obsess and stress over our budget and spending so much that it seemed to control him. After I came home from the store, he resorted to making remarks like, "Do you really need another candle? Don't you have tons already?" Did I need a dollar candle? Maybe not, but it somehow helped me retain a small part of my former self as an independent woman. I worked hard to make ends meet, cutting coupons and saving where we could. I also didn't feel as if my role as a caregiver should be devalued! Did you know one annual study[1] found that in 2019 the average stay-at-home mom would make a median salary of $178,201 if she was paid for her job duties? I wasn't accustomed to asking for an allowance or feeling like it was only "his" money to spend. He got a coffee on the way to work, so why couldn't I buy a little candle? I shouldn't have to operate under the mindset of doing this wonderful thing for our family; being such a big part of our kids' upbringing reduces me to be a financial burden. But his comments made me feel incredibly guilty. As if I was simply wasting money when we had the utility bill coming up for the first month of air-conditioned summer days.

These comments and feelings hit me hard. We were both full of resentment while lacking in understanding, and it sucked.

The understanding part is critical. To have empathy, you need to understand. The very definition of empathy is "the ability to understand and share the feelings of another." Unfortunately, we failed to see what the other person's daily routine was indeed like, looking through rose-colored glasses at each other's distinctive roles. My husband frequently liked to say, "oh, it must be nice to sit and relax at the pool all day." This phrase might as well have been a slap in the face. If only he knew the amount of preparation, sweat, and tears that went into getting three kids to the pool, especially when some of them were barely walking age. Once at the pool, I irritatedly begged my oldest to stop asking when it was time to go into the big pool. I desperately tried to keep my youngest tiny daredevil from drowning and repeatedly explained to my middle child that we didn't come to the pool to eat snacks. In between stopping meltdowns and saving lives, I had the joyous task of applying sunscreen to three little wiggling octopi and reapplying throughout the day. After our day of fun, we had to tackle the arduous task of changing in a locker room without dropping our dry, clean clothes in puddles of water. At home, I had to unpack, wash, and dry everything before trying to manage a few of the chores that didn't get done while I was away. While I did enjoy seeing my kids splash in the pool and enjoy the summer sun's rays, relaxing was far from how I would describe my day.

I would encourage the partners of stay-at-home parents to withhold all judgment. In many cases, you don't have a clue what happened while you were away at work. Does the house look the same as when you left? That pile of crumbs under the highchair is probably only the tip of the iceberg when it comes to the day's actual occurrences. From the time you leave to when you come home, hundreds of messes were made and subsequently cleaned up. Your partner probably isn't lounging all day but doing their best just to keep their head above water in a sea of toys, spilled milk, and squashed playdough. It took a while for my husband and me to start reserving our judgment and truly start listening to one another.

I'm sad to admit that we butted heads and argued for a couple of years about who is the harder-working (read: better) parent. Finally, we decided to hash it out by making a list. I made a list of all the things that frustrated me about what he did or didn't do. For a couple of hours here and there, I toiled away at my list of grievances. Yes, you read that right, *hours*. By the time I was done, the list was a couple of pages long. But it was worth it. Vindicated by my list, I was lighter and able to let go of everything I had been holding onto. Past situations that I felt still needed closure, present troubles, and future fears. He made a list too. Now, here is one of the most important parts, we got a sitter. The poor girl was probably a bit confused when we didn't head out for a date night. Instead, we armed ourselves with a beverage of choice, our pages-long list of our spouse's criminal actions, and headed out to our patio. She didn't know what she had signed up for! But we wanted to be able to hear each other, listen without interruptions, and have sacred grown-up time devoted to what felt like saving our marriage.

Kids handled and nerves fortified, we sat down for what seemed like a make-or-break discussion. I was angry, but I was also nervous. I wanted things to change, and I *needed* something to change. I couldn't stay at home with our kids if my sanity, health, and marriage continued to suffer as a result. We agreed and promised not to comment or interrupt the other person until they were completely finished. We decided not to silently stew and formulate barbed comebacks as the other person spoke but to listen and think for a bit before responding. I was relieved, and you'll be relieved to know that it went surprisingly well. We uncovered our main issues: not enough alone time, not enough sex, feelings of resentment, and thinking the other was not doing enough for the family.

I'm sure these are common in almost every relationship, no matter what the couple's working lives look like. With everything out in the open, we felt pretty silly that we let things go on like this for so long. We were determined to improve the state of our marriage, our home, and both our sanity. We made a list of the top ten things the other person could do to help. My list centered around keeping the kids entertained so I could have some time to myself. His list pertained to ways I could show more appreciation and attraction to him. Before becoming a stay-at-home mom, I didn't face much pressure in my job. And that's just it; when I did experience pressure, it usually wasn't around my husband but at work. I wasn't prepared for who I would become under pressure, and my husband wasn't well-versed in how I handled pressure or how to support me through challenging times. As a result, my actions were foreign to him and, needless to say, a bit confusing. His male brain went straight to an affair. He thought I was pulling away from him because I was finding love in someone else's arms. This was so far from the truth. The thought of having *anyone* physically touching me, let alone a stranger, was enough to send me into a spiral, physically brushing off my arms as if to shed the touch of another human. I was touched out big time. I was also experiencing panic attacks. Naturally, he thought something was seriously wrong (which it kind of was), which made him stressed even more. This was especially torturous for him when he was at work and couldn't see how I was acting or responding. He would let his imagination get the best of him. Do you see how much this lack of communication and understanding impacted every part of our lives?

Neither of us was foolish or wrong. I admittedly wasn't the best at showing him affection. I thought that he should just know how much I care for and appreciate him. I mean, we were still married, right? And after spending all day with the kids I often felt seriously touched out by the time he came home. He needed to empathize a bit more with my situation, and if possible, put his own desires on hold for a minute to make sure that I felt supported emotionally and mentally. The bottom line was that we each needed to be more aware of making one another feel more secure and more loved and openly communicate those wants, desires, needs, and feelings to one another.

It's effortless for a stay-at-home parent and the spouse of a stay-at-home parent to pass judgment on one another. While the now-at-home parent probably remembers the difficulties of working outside the home, they may have difficulty reconciling those struggles, especially with their new role that is often overwhelming and exhausting. Staying at home with your kids is hard. While it may not be open heart surgery hard, or hosting live television hard, it's a unique breed of difficulty. A day in and day out relentlessness that slowly wears on you both mentally and physically. My husband may have wanted to relax when he came home. I remember working long hours on my feet as a CNA, but that seemed paltry to what I had just experienced all day. He couldn't understand why I just *needed* him to take the kids. Tasks that were once simple were no longer simple. I couldn't even perform the most basic human tasks, like going to the bathroom without worrying about a child trying to swim in the fish tank or paint the walls with diaper cream. Want to take the trash to the end of the drive? Better strap the kids in a stroller because there is no way you can leave them unattended for sixty seconds. Nothing is simple. Ever. Even when my husband was home, I was the go-to parent. If mom was the person they turned to all day long, she became the de facto parent even when dad was around. My toddler would walk from the kitchen, where his dad was sitting, to my bedroom upstairs simply to ask me for a glass of water. "YOUR FATHER IS RIGHT THERE!" the incredulous darts shooting out from my eyeballs read. Aside from him not understanding why I needed a break, another point of contention was the state of the house. He went to work, and his colleagues left him alone to complete his tasks and finish projects. I went to "work" when my kids woke up, and productivity might as well have been thrown out the window. Productivity doesn't exist with little kids. You can throw the laundry in the machine, but you might as well forget about folding. Emails, phone calls, paying bills, not until nap time (if that even happens!). Actual productivity, or consistent blocks of time set aside to accomplish tasks, doesn't mesh with being a stay-at-home parent of little children. Part of that stems from what being a "good" stay-at-home parent means in today's society. That ideology doesn't leave room for housekeeping or financial managing or any of the other stuff June Cleaver routinely did. Stay-at-home parents are expected to be continuously involved with all aspects of their children's development. Pinterest parents who teach, play and nurture their children in the most hands-on way possible. If housework and 21st-century stay-at-home parent were on a dating show, they would be deemed incompatible. It isn't easy for stay-at-home parents to voice these things, just as it can be difficult for parents who work outside of the home to understand and empathize.

A dear friend of mine and her husband used to argue about how he never helped around the house whenever he had free time. His replies were always along the lines of "you never ask me," "if you need help, just tell me what to do," "I don't know what you need help with if you don't tell me and I don't want to mess up your flow." The problem was her "flow" was, in fact, her slowly drowning in a sea of housework. She wasn't staying ahead of the current, but sinking. They had this same argument time and time again for years. Until one day, he started asking, "how can I help you" "what can I take off your plate?" It was so much easier for her to give him a task, like unloading the dishwasher or folding the clean laundry, than it was for her to actively seek him out and ask him to do those things. It seems to be far easier to delegate a task when someone asks if you need help than to reach out and ask for help. Communication is key, my friends. This small change has drastically altered their relationship in a positive way.

A couple's relationship often takes a backseat to children. Still, it is crucial to keep the lines of communication open as much as possible. Also, know you will likely let these lines break down occasionally and will have to put in honest hard work to get things back in order. You will probably argue and quarrel and feel resentment for each other at times. Transition is difficult for everyone involved. However, you and your partner are a team. You rely on each other to be a support system; an ear to listen, a shoulder to cry on, and a person to help pick up the slack. To be successful as a stay-at-home parent, you need your partner on board, physically, mentally, and emotionally. The only way to know where each other stands is by communicating. I find relief in journaling. Don't let me fool you; my process isn't as relaxing and meditative as it sounds. Instead, I frequently jot down my thoughts and frustrations. Simply getting things out of my head and onto paper helps me manage the daily stress. It also helps me to reflect so that if my husband asks what's going on with me? I can clue him in as to how I am feeling.

Earlier in the chapter, I discussed how one of our significant flaws in my transition to being a stay-at-home mom was that neither of us knew what to expect. Once we were immersed in our new roles, quite unhappily, and decided to air our grievances, we had a fantastic idea. We wrote job descriptions. We each defined our new roles. This helped us manage our expectations, reserve our judgments, and create equality among our duties. Different things work for other families. I have a girlfriend who is a stay-at-home mom. She takes care of the children, cooks, and cleans during the day, but as soon as her husband gets home, he takes over all those tasks. We know another family in which the father works full time, attends school full time, and is in the Army National Guard. The mother stays at home and is in charge of the children, cooking, and cleaning at all times. The arrangement that works for their family is that he provides income and works towards an advanced degree to provide additional income one day, hopefully. In return, she manages everything within the home. This works for them; everyone is happy, and all tasks get taken care of. I take care of the kids during the day in our family, but my husband takes over when he gets home. I still do all the cooking and cleaning. It was never really the chores that got to me, but the feeling of being touched-out. What mattered most to me was that my husband provided me with some sort of alone time away from our kids. It would help if you decided what a stay-at-home mom looks like for your family. As the stay-at-home parent, are you strictly in charge of taking care of the kids, or are you also responsible for all the housework? Are you going to share meal planning and preparing responsibilities, or will you already have that done when your partner gets home from work? Some people enjoy the traditional roles of being a housewife. In contrast, others think that's antiquated, and they are strictly a stay-at-home mom, not a housewife. When this journey begins, you need to be on the same page as your partner, or the transition probably won't be successful. Even if you still aren't sure what to expect or don't have a clear picture of what your roles will look like, you and your partner can still be a team. Constantly communicate and be open to change. If something isn't working, discuss it and make a plan on how to fix it. Find what works for your family in terms of childcare and chore duties. And one final piece of advice? At the end of the day, no one will care if you had time to scrub the shower. There is always tomorrow. If your partner says otherwise, there's the Clorox and the brush, have at it.

4

FAMILY, FRIENDS, AND FELLOW DOMESTIC ENGINEERS - BUILDING YOUR SUPPORT SYSTEM

It takes a village is one of the most accurate phrases I have ever heard. It comes from an African proverb that means that a whole community of people must provide for and interact positively with a child to grow, learn, and experience a safe and healthy environment. Unfortunately, many of us have become family units wholly removed from our villages. There's nothing wrong with being strong and independent, but sometimes you need to lean on others for support. I mean, the song Independent Woman is sung by Destiny's Child, a group of three women who you better believe relied on each other for encouragement, help, and a shoulder to cry on. When we try to go it alone, it's not only our children who will miss out on the rich environment of a community and suffer the effects of being isolated; it's us, parents, too.

A robust support system is everything when you are a stay-at-home mom. The times and ways in which I have relied on my friends and family are innumerable. Sometimes you need someone to vent to who can empathize with what you are going through and listen to your frustrations. You need friends who will help you laugh through the tears when your child decides to paint with lipstick on your non-washable sectional. A family who can step in to watch your other kids while you take the feverish toddler to the doctor. Having people who understand that you need support is crucial. Support even when it means having broken conversations between shouting to your demanding teenager. Sending long overdue texts that got lost between cooking dinner and bedtime routines. Someone who knows that you can't call them back later when you're not busy because, frankly, that time doesn't exist. Personally, my best forms of support listen, agree, tell me how great of a mother I am, even when I sound like a raving lunatic. They see me at my best, but more often at my worst. They don't judge the state of my house or my physical self. Even when I greet them with one soaked nursing pad popping out of my shirt to say "hello" and a smear of unidentifiable brown on my yoga pants. Instead, they laugh and cry with me.

They occupy my kiddos so that I can take a shower. They show up in an emergency when there's no one to watch my kids at 2 am. They understand that grocery shopping alone is a treat and will invite my kids over so that I can make the trip sans children. They commiserate with me when I relay the story of abandoning a full shopping cart because my child had an epic temper tantrum over yellow and not brown bananas. They're irreplaceable, and their support is inexhaustible.

I didn't start with a kickass support system though. When you transition to becoming a stay-at-home mom, your existing support network essentially becomes "service interrupted." Those co-workers who frequently lend an ear while you complain about your commute to work suddenly become your husband who doesn't understand how hard it is to do one load of laundry when you're home all day, "*just* watching the kids." Your boss is now a demanding toddler with insane project deadlines and a penchant for rolling on the floor screaming when they aren't met, something your fellow work outside the home mothers just can't quite sympathize with. What I am saying is that our best supporters are typically those who know what we are going through. They're in the trenches with us, fighting the same daily battles. When you become a stay-at-home mom, your entire situation changes. Your routine, priorities, and experiences are drastically different. The family members and friends who once totally understood where you were coming from might as well now be on a different planet speaking a foreign language. I'm not saying that you have to cut ties with all your old pals and join a stay-at-home mom cult; just don't be surprised if you find it harder to connect with others who aren't or have never been a stay-at-home parent. Many stay-at-home parents find that their sense of self and identity changes when they transition to staying home. This includes the people you once surrounded yourself with and leaned on for support.

The biggest takeaway here is to make sure you do whatever you need to make your support system happen. Do not be afraid to ask for help. Do not be embarrassed to reach out. Please do not fool yourself into thinking you can go it alone. The stronger your support system, the less chance you have of getting stay-at-home mom burnout. I can not tell you how often I have shown up at a friend or family member's house and dropped off my kids. Sometimes, it was an emergency that urgently needed my attention. Other times it was because if I did not have thirty minutes to myself at precisely that moment, I would end up in a padded cell. I would do and have done the same for them. Your partner will probably be around, yes, but he can't and should not be your only form of support. If you read the previous chapter, you see how close I was to buckling under the pressure, and my husband was home every morning and evening. It isn't fair to you or your partner to expect them to be your sole supporter. What's worse, though, is if you try to hold down the fort, raise the kids, and be a model wife while keeping your struggles, fears, and feelings to yourself. Stay-at-home mom burnout is a real thing and quickly becoming a more common issue. The grueling monotony of the day can be oppressive. When your eyes crack open in the morning, not due to an alarm clock but instead the wails of your toddler, you know full well what to expect. Butts to wipe, messes to clean, meals to prepare, chores to tackle.

A day spent trying to get the house looking like it did when your partner left, let alone trying to get any real work done. Failed to-do lists, no definite goals you're moving towards, and the drudgery of an often thankless routine can lead to feelings of sadness, disappointment, and depression. Previously I've talked about the feelings of no escape. These are especially exacerbated when you don't have friends to meet for a playdate, family to watch your children every once in a while, or even someone you can shoot off an SOS text to. Imagine cabin fever on steroids. Maybe you don't have to imagine it; maybe you're in the never-ending cycle of dirty dishes, dirty diapers, and dirty comments about how grateful you should be that you get to stay home all day. While many of us stay-at-home moms feel sad and isolated now and again, for some of us, it goes much deeper. The feelings when people remark about your lack of a real job (I now tell people I am a domestic engineer), the comments your partner makes when the house looks worse than it did before he left, the daily grind that is really, truly, a grind. It can be enough to make you want to hide under the covers and never come out! A support system won't make these feelings magically go away, but it can help. Your support team will include friends who validate your feelings, people who understand your struggles, and those who make you feel like you're a real person, somebody, and not just "mom." With friends, you'll probably still be flailing in the ocean of at-home motherhood, but at least you won't be sinking, and better yet, you won't be out to sea alone.

It's easy to isolate yourself as a stay-at-home parent. I mean, it's in the job description, you don't get out much, you *stay at home*. Even when you do leave the house for a few precious moments, you're probably running to the grocery store or dropping off a package, not meeting up with friends. The more you withdraw from others, the more your support group dwindles. Now is when you need friends and family more than ever! So how do you find friends who get you and can help you because they *are* you? Fellow stay-at-home parents, from inexperienced to veteran?

Starting virtually can be a great option. If you have just moved or are not comfortable just walking up to a fellow mom at the park, social media can help! I know, I know, the internet is mainly terrible, but I'll admit that it does have some benefits. On popular social media platforms, you can search for local mom groups. You can join them virtually, then learn about and attend in-person events as you become more comfortable. Online groups that rarely meet in person and consist of people spread out all over the globe can be another excellent resource. They can provide an ear to listen to if you need to vent or a sounding board to bounce ideas off. Commonly they're made up of both new and expert stay-at-home parents that can occasionally offer some pretty solid advice, like why your kid may have a weird rash in his armpits. It can be reassuring to know that you are not alone and to have guidance at your fingertips. However, I urge you not to let your support system be only virtual. You need a group of people who you can show up on their doorstep wearing a t-shirt with snot smears and holding a baby with a diaper bag, and they'll ask, "what do you need?" instead of "what the heck?" To find your flesh and bone stay-at-home besties, check out libraries, parks, community centers, and other places where parents of children congregate.

Your local library likely has a variety of activities to join during the week that are completely free to you, such as toddler storytime or babygarten. Nearby parks are a great way to meet fellow parents, especially if you go during the day. Chances are, if a mom or dad is there midday with their kids, then they are a stay home parent. Coffee shops, indoor playscapes, and other activity centers are a bit hit and miss when it comes to finding fellow stay-at-homer's, but they're worth a try too! Soon enough, you will find someone you gel with and can hopefully start building a friendship. If you are not an outgoing conversationalist, don't worry, someone else probably will be. My kids also have a wonderful habit of starting conversations for me, whether they're putting sand down their pants and another mom spots them first, or they're being sweet to a fellow child on the playground. Many times my crazy kiddos have opened the door to friendly conversations with their silly antics. I happened to meet two of my best mom-friends simply by being in the right place at the right time, and you can bet both of these places were popular parent/children hangouts. Swim lessons was the sight of our bestie beginnings, if you will. I like to consider myself a social butterfly. Still, my kids will tell you that I will talk to anyone, even the person behind us in the grocery line. My now best friend was shy and quiet. I actually struck up a conversation with her mother, who had accompanied her to swim lessons. After a while, my introverted friend slowly opened up during our weekly meetings at the pool and felt comfortable enough to accept my invitation to a play-date. The rest is history! We are now each other's biggest cheerleaders, and my kids even call her mom "grandma." Putting yourself out there is the first step. You don't have anything to lose, but you do have everything to gain. I am so adamant about having a solid support system because rates of depression among stay-at-home mothers are trending upwards.[1]

While I am not proposing the idea that having a support system will prevent depression or that not having a support system will make you depressed; I do believe that having a group of friends and family who can be there for you during your darkest moments and get you the help you need is essential. Postpartum depression is gaining the recognition and resources it deserves. According to the American Pregnancy Association[2]postpartum depression occurs between birth and one year postpartum. However, moms can still experience depression beyond one year postpartum. This type of depression among mothers, especially stay-at-home moms, commonly isn't as widely recognized. Some of the signs and symptoms of depression are not always obvious. Depression can be sneaky and very serious. Fatigue and changes in your sleep habits are normal after having kids, as are feelings of isolation and loneliness when you transition to becoming a stay-at-home mom. How do you know if your lack of enthusiasm for facing the day is because you had a rough night with the baby or could be something more? Some characteristics of depression are more noticeable, like persistent sadness and drastic weight changes. But those suffering from depression can also do so in silence. This might be even more true of mothers who believe they should have it all together, all the time. I am no stranger to the feeling of carrying the world's weight on my shoulders and wondering if I let just one ball drop, what will happen to my family? Many moms struggling with depression appear competent because they take care of their children and their home, like a well-oiled machine that never stops. A common symptom reported by depressed mothers is irritability. After doing all the things on my list, I'm usually irritable by the end of the day. Who wouldn't be? That is why the symptoms can be so hard to spot. Experts don't yet know the root cause of depression, but when it comes to mothers, they suspect that their exhaustive duties and the multiple demands they face may play a role. Even though mental health issues can run in families, environmental and situational factors can have an effect too. When you think about it, chronic stress has been shown to contribute to depression, and what is more stressful than the grueling marathon of motherhood?

It isn't unusual for women to fear that seeking help for mental health issues shows weakness or a bad mother. Stress and anxiety are widespread in families with young children. Especially now with social media picture-perfect moments and Pinterest-moms being the norm. Worries about not measuring up or being able to make every moment of your little one's childhood special are enough to make anyone go into a tailspin. Every time I go on the internet to plan a birthday party for one of my kids, I get so stressed that I can't sleep. Scrolling through page after page of party ideas, I focus on how unique and tied together everything looks. How much did they spend on that cake? How long did it take them to plan and set up three different activity stations for a group of fifteen rambunctious elementary schoolers? How in the heck will I make a bulldozer out of balloons and rent an elephant in three weeks? My goodie bags have to include an Ipad and a personalized case with coordinating app recommendations? Who in the world can afford that? I get so overwhelmed that I end up wasting all my time crying in a pillow, then resorting to tying some balloons on a couple of chairs and making a cake from a box. And surprise, surprise; my kid has the time of his five-year-old life! I love the phrase, "the fact that you worry about being a good mom means you already are one." Don't believe the lie that seeking help for your mental health makes you any less of an amazing mother. I urge you to research the topic of depression more and learn about the symptoms. You can even involve your partner. This way, you and those close to you can be aware of the signs to watch out for.

I don't claim to be a medical professional. Still, my mama instinct tells me (and I know firsthand) that a robust support system helps stay-at-home parents both mentally and physically. Knowing that someone is waiting for you to walk the park trails with them holds you accountable. It gets you out of the house, forces you into a "check-in" with your friends or family, and gets your body moving. Knowing someone has your back should an emergency come up or you have a particularly bad day, gives you the confidence and security to take on another day of cleaning, cooking, playing, teaching, and nurturing your children. Having a network of people who can provide emotional support and "real-world" support can significantly reduce your stress and help improve your maternal health. And as they say, "when mama's happy, everybody's happy"!

5

THE REASON FOR ROUTINES, SCHEDULING FOR YOUR SANITY

Before becoming a stay-at-home mom, you may have approached the weekend with a mix of excitement and dread. As you checked off the days on your calendar, you wondered what Saturday and Sunday might hold. There were two possibilities. In one version, you complete the chores that had piled up by late morning, after which you would prepare a simple lunch that every kid would eat without complaint. Then, you could spend the afternoon playing make-believe or building a fort, perhaps getting a jog in while your partner took the kids to the park. Finally, in the evening, everyone would pile onto the couch to pick a movie without bickering or complaining about who got to choose last time, and you would go to bed at peace with the world. Version number two was a live reenactment of the movie Gremlins while you suffer through housework that never ends. So when you transitioned to a role in which you were home with your kids every day instead of just the weekends, it may have been a little worrisome. What if they morphed into feral animals Monday through Friday? What if every day was like your worst weekend? Whether you are anxious over your children's behavior or you believe there's no way you can get all the things done without your partner around to watch the kids or both; there is a solution to your problem. The answer is routine, routine, routine.

There are two schools of thought when it comes to routine. Free-spirit versus structured. I tend to fall somewhere in the middle. I don't need to direct my child's every move, but I do need some semblance of a pattern to plan when to pay bills, make phone calls, and tackle the odd household job. It's true; having a routine for my kids is partly for me. But it is beneficial for them too. They, to a point, know what to expect each day. When they wake up, we head downstairs for breakfast at the table while I unload the dishwasher. Do I have them up at 6 am sharp each morning? No. Do I wake them up one morning and decide to heck with breakfast we're going to the park? Also no. I don't treat staying at home like one long vacation and throwing routine out the window, but I don't regiment their minutes like a drill sergeant either. A balance of child-led self-direction and mom-imposed structure works best for my family.

In my experience, I have noticed that most children thrive off of a consistent routine. This is due to a few reasons. First, it can provide them with a sense of security in a constantly changing world and in which their control is quite limited. They know what to expect, and clear expectations can cut down on arguing. Routines and children's part in them can strengthen their self-confidence. And, having a schedule that includes important family moments can facilitate bonding (who said routines couldn't include fun?). Many of these things apply to parents too. You know what to expect. You have a sense of security. Seeing your child become independent and confident boosts your belief that maybe you're getting the hang of this motherhood thing. Finally, reducing stress for both parents and children is a massive benefit of a routine. You don't have to wonder when you will have time to clean, cook, or throw in a load of laundry when you pencil in downtime or a nap consistently each day. This can help tremendously, improving your mood with your kids and your partner. My stay-at-home schedule keeps me sane. Without it, I ping pong between two personality traits, type-A and apathetic, due to being overwhelmed. That was perhaps one of the most complex parts of my transition, knowing that I had a lot to get done but that an infant and a toddler would direct my days. For a while, I floundered. Well, in reality, I ran around like a chicken with my head cut off. I was bouncing from task to task, getting one kid up just as I put the other down (bye-bye free time). In earlier chapters, I attribute some of my feelings to my lack of routine when I was a stay-at-home newbie.

Thankfully, the more days my kids and I experienced together, the more we sort of fell into a routine. So even though I seem like I am preaching a schedule (which I am), I am also all for letting your little one's guide elements of your plan and dictate some of your schedule priorities. If I could go back to my former self knowing what I know now as a veteran stay-at-homer, here is what I would advise.

Let's make a schedule. First, start with priorities, namely, sleep. Sleep is one of the things that cannot change, or at least it shouldn't! You need rest, and your kids need sleep. We *all* need sleep, sister. Sleep is also one of those things that there isn't any way around. Without naps, your kids get cranky; adults get cranky without at least six to eight hours. It wouldn't be fair to anyone's sanity not to give naps, bedtime, and wake-up an esteemed place within your scheduling priorities. In that same vein, mealtimes, especially with young kids, don't vary too much and certainly cannot be skipped. These two essentials, sleeping, and eating should help dictate the rest of your schedule. Your schedule will also likely be structured around external factors, such as school drop-off and activity hours at the library. You don't have any accurate control over these things, so it is best to give them high priority when creating your schedule.

In addition to times, I also like to think about moods when making my schedule. When am I most productive? When are my kids most open to learning or doing tasks that may not be the most "fun"? Incorporating you and your children's natural moods and "flow" into your day will help everything go along much more smoothly. I found that I truly benefit from alone time when the kids are asleep at the end of the day. I often get a second wind of motivation and feel like I can tackle a workout, a writing project, or just another thing on my to-do list late in the evening. The knowledge that my kids are asleep for a solid chunk of hours and usually won't wake up and interrupt my grind allows me to work confidently without pressure or anxiety. Trying to wake up early before my kids arise to get things done is not my jam. Some people are the opposite, and they are the most productive in the morning. They work the best under pressure and can hop out of bed and get to it, racing to beat the deadline that is their kids scampering down the stairs. Others thrive during that afternoon nap block. Your schedule is all about what works best for you and your family.

Now that you have your priorities and your list of items that don't vary much from day to day, or week to week, let's begin drafting our schedule in earnest. I find that organizing our days into time slots works well. I get for some that this may be too rigid, but I promise, I'm not going to be encouraging you to carry around a stopwatch and enforce these time slots like a drill sergeant. Instead, you will be using them as a guide. The framework of your day will be your "unchanging" tasks, like getting a child on the bus or meeting for a weekly playgroup. Once you plug in these activities, you will be left with your available times. These unscheduled hours are perfect for when you need to schedule a doctor's appointment, meet with a fellow mom at the park, or engage in whatever your little one feels like that day. For you, as a parent, you can also get a good idea of when you will have time to complete to-do's on your list, from making phone calls to doing the dishes. I believe that consistency is key to overcoming domestic challenges. Before I found a routine that worked, our days could only be described as chaotic. I would try to start something before my kids woke up, then I would feel resentful when I had to stop my work to prepare breakfast and get them ready for the day. We would do an activity that took way longer than I expected, only to remember afterward that I still had to go grocery shopping. Our trip to the store would inevitably run into my kid's afternoon nap which resulted in a cranky toddler and a frazzled mom running through the aisles. I was less apt to add anything to our day, like storytime events or gym class, because I didn't have a solid idea of who was doing what when. A schedule helped to expand our horizons and benefited my children. Once I knew what each day's plan was, I could see, "Yes! We could meet for little learners every Tuesday at the community center" and "Sure! We do have a block of time for swim lessons on Thursday mornings!" It also helped me stay consistently on top of domestic challenges (at least for the most part).

Our family's day starts with a morning routine scheduled from 7:00 to 8:00. This includes getting dressed, combing hair, brushing teeth, eating breakfast, the everyday tasks we humans engage in after rolling out of bed. No matter what, I always try to get up and get everyone dressed and fed around the same time each day. It is a great habit to have, not to mention good practice for school-aged children and having a bus to catch. It also helps start our day off with a sense of assurance and regularity, and my kids know what to expect. Then, the kiddos usually have a little bit of free choice playtime to do puzzles, games, books, blocks, and the like. Generally, a few days a week, our mornings will have a planned activity with others. On the days that don't have an event, I base our schedule on my children's moods. By late morning, after their free choice time, if they had lots of energy and needed to expend it, then this is when I penciled in our outdoor time or playtime. It doesn't have to be a specific event; for example, it might be outdoor play at a park one day, indoor play at a trampoline park with friends the next. Figure out when your children are the most active and plan outdoor/active play for that period. As long as you have the time blocked off, you can go into details later. Next, we would eat lunch, and then a large part of the afternoon was occupied with naps or quiet time. When my children were young, I scheduled quiet time before naps to help them wind down and know that sleep is coming soon. We would read a book or maybe talk about our favorite part of the morning. It was a great pause and helped my kids transition into naptime. Speaking of naps, I would always plan my cleaning tasks for their nap times. As my kids have gotten older and more independent, I can clean while they entertain themselves. When they were young, household chores were usually best handled when they were asleep. You can divide your domestic duty schedule by tasks or by rooms over the course of the week, whatever you prefer. For example, you can mop all the floors Monday, dust every room Tuesday, collect all the garbage Wednesday, change all the bed linens Thursday, scrub all the toilets Friday. If going room by room is what works better for you, your schedule may look something like bathrooms Monday, living room Tuesday, office Wednesday, bedrooms Thursday, playroom Friday. I never schedule laundry or dishes. I do those in every spare minute of every day. I can quickly unload the dishwasher while the kids are eating breakfast or fold clothes while they are content watching a show or playing a game. If I tried to schedule these things, we would never have any clean clothes to wear or clean dishes to eat off. My husband knows that once he gets home from work, I go somewhere and take thirty minutes for myself. This is one of my planned momma-alone-time blocks. Sometimes I go for a walk, or a drive, or take a bath, or sit on the patio with wine. What I do usually depends on how crazy the day was and what my mood is like. Our evenings were pretty relaxed before the kids were school-aged; we ate dinner, had some family time, went through our whole bedtime routine, and then my husband and I had a little bit of freedom. I loved that even with this "loose" schedule, there seemed to be less of a fight when it came to nap times and bedtime, and we adults were nearly guaranteed an hour of kid-free time starting around

8:00 each night.

I have a daily planner to record all my details, but you can use anything you'd like. A planner, a notebook, a spreadsheet, your phone's calendar, whatever works best for you. Just make sure to stick with one. There is nothing worse than having your kids' schedules written in one place, appointments in another, and your to-do list is crumpled in the bottom of your purse. When you don't keep everything together, you will forget appointments, get off schedule, and most likely, you and/or the kids will end up having a meltdown.

Things will change as the children get older, nap times will become shorter, playdates will become longer, and afterschool activities will begin. Give yourself grace while adjusting to a new schedule, as it will happen quite a few times over the years. Friends who were parents of older children always told me, wait until they are in elementary school and travel sports begin, or middle school, and they start wanting you to drive them everywhere to meet friends. Then, in high school, they start drama club and band, and the list goes on. I'm not a fan of the whole "just wait" doomsday phrase of motherhood, but your schedule really will go through some massive shifts as your children get older. You won't be busier per se, but the activities your middle schooler's schedule is consumed with will be drastically different than when they were a toddler. Of course, it is easier said than done, but I highly advise going with the flow and tweaking your schedule to allow for these new and exciting changes. No matter what stage of life you are in, there will always be challenges and routine interruptions like vacations and illnesses. But I encourage you to get back to the routine as soon as you can. My children are a bit older now, so I have been more flexible with their schedules over the summer. However, as soon as school starts, it's back to the routine. It is much easier when things are planned out.

Every Sunday, I make time to sit down and figure out my upcoming week. I find that Sunday is the ideal time for me to do this. Usually, by that point, I have a pretty good handle on what the coming week has in store. My husband is home to watch the kids, so I have a few moments to myself. Planning my schedule on Sunday gives me an incredible feeling of satisfaction, knowing that I am prepared for what's to come and won't be blindsided (hopefully). You can do it any day that you like though. I look at my calendar, planner, emails, text messages, etc., and write down everything planned for the upcoming week. My personal favorite planner has vertical time slots for each day, so it's easier for me to stick to my schedule. Still, a piece of notebook paper or virtual sheet will work just fine. Once I have all my appointments moved from my monthly calendar to my weekly schedule and all of our planned playdates, activities, and the like, I can start filling in the blanks with household chores and other things that may be fun, educational, or seasonal in the open spaces. If this sounds a bit overwhelming, don't panic. You don't need to fill up the days. It is okay to have open spaces for child-led activities, free time, or simply breathing room. Keep in mind that one of your time slots can be for relaxing or doing a hobby you enjoy. Remember, you make the rules.

While I'm scheduling my week, I also like to make my meal plan. This is a perfect time because you can see what nights you have extracurriculars and will have to leave the house early or will get home late. If your husband has a meeting on Thursday, you can plan that pasta dish that you love but he doesn't like. Having a meal plan is incredibly important to a stay-at-home mom's success. I've been advocating meal planning since the "Having a Budget" chapter in the beginning. With only one income, you need to be careful to stick to a grocery budget. There's generally no wiggle room to go out to dinner when you can't think of anything to cook. Plan your meals, and the problem is solved! I may also use this scheduling time to keep up with my inventory, another big part of meal planning. For example, if I have beef in the freezer, I will plan a taco night, then write on my schedule "take beef from the freezer" so I remember to prep for that night's dinner. However, I recommend keeping a spare frozen pizza on hand for nights you don't feel like cooking the elaborate meal you planned earlier in the week.

Having a schedule is not meant to stress you out more. Start with your necessities, then add extras and downtime. Suppose it turns out to be too much; back off some. Your schedule will likely evolve. It doesn't have to be perfect from the get-go, or ever really. Suppose your plan falls to pieces during the day; that's fine too. This is not set in stone, and your adherence to it is not measured by how good of a mother you are. Having a schedule and a routine is helpful but not required. When you are a stay-at-home parent, you are the boss. It is now your job to figure out what to do. For some people, the thought of that is stressful and can be overwhelming. If you are a take-charge kind of person, you will be great at this. If you are not, I am sure you soon will be and will end up impressing yourself. Give yourself grace if you have let the schedule slip for a day or forty. Simply start again; rarely do people stick with a new routine the first time they try it out. Heck, I've tried to go to the gym weekly, and I haven't managed to stick with that routine for years. I keep trying though! Just like I know that getting my butt on that treadmill would be excellent for my health, I also know that having a scheduled day as a stay-at-home mom can be a lot easier than a free for all, even if it does take a little bit of planning and work. Here is an example of the style of planner I use. There are so many options out there. Find what works for you!

Daily Planner

M T W T F S S

Date:

To-Do List

Priorities

Notes

7:00

8:00

9:00

10:00

11:00

12:00

1:00

2:00

3:00

4:00

5:00

6:00

7:00

8:00

9:00

6

EXPECT THE UNEXPECTED

Congratulations! You have a routine! All's right with the world, and your days will now go off without a hitch! Wrong. Life, or more accurately a tiny human, has a way of disrupting even the most well-laid plans. So be prepared to be unprepared.

For a while, the local park was my arch enemy, my biggest foe, the site of a battle I could never seem to win. It never failed; I would spend time getting the kids ready, feeding them breakfast or lunch, and dressing them appropriately for the weather. I would carefully pack everything we could possibly need; snacks, sunscreen, a few toys for the baby, hats, jackets, you name it, it was shoved within the depths of my bag. Then I would wrestle our gear into the trunk of my van; two bikes plus helmets, a stroller, and the clip-on umbrella for good measure. This was going to be great, nay fantastic! I was so well equipped to handle whatever could come my way. It was my kiddos, and I versus the elements, and this mama wasn't about to let anything ruin her outdoor playtime. But you see, I was mistaken. It was never us versus the environment, at least not the outdoor environment. It was always us pitted against my child's gastrointestinal environment, their ability to try and hold it as we made a mad dash to the bathroom. We never made it. It was as sure as the sun rising each morning; nearly every trip to the park resulted in a poop explosion.

Sure, I had extra clothes, but I didn't have an extra car seat or stroller when the accidents occurred. They were safely and securely buckled into their five-point harnesses, like mini-astronauts ready for a space flight. Unfortunately, unlike those space travelers, my children did not have suits with built-in lavatory systems. When it wasn't poop covering a necessary baby gear item, it was the threat of more poop to come. We would inevitably have to pack up and head home. After a sprint to the bathrooms, they would complain of an upset stomach, and just the thought of having to try to furiously corral all my other kiddos so we could race to the stall again was enough to have me packing it in. It just seemed like my kids' bowels had it out for me and my park plan. Every. Single. Time.

The park wasn't the only place my schedule would sometimes go awry. A quick trip to the grocery store? How about being stuck in a traffic jam with hungry kids who all need to pee instead. A fantastic day at the farm center? Try riding home mid-afternoon with wet, dirty, uncomfortable, and incessantly complaining children. Because unbeknownst to me, there was a sandbox playground complete with a water feature installed in the play area.

I have become a master motherhood prepper over the years. I have an emergency potty in my van lined with a plastic bag ready for a quick tie-up. I travel with a roll of disposable dirty diaper bags at all times. They come in handy as puke bags, dirty clothes bags, soiled shoe bags, and so much more. I have a first aid kit that would put the military to shame.

I have experienced quite a few van mishaps. I have had a child throw up directly into an open bag of groceries just purchased from the supermarket. I have had a child cover a car seat in a shade of yellow-green previously unidentified by Pantone. I have had my preparation skills, and resiliency tested more times than I care to admit. Each time my packing list grew by another item or two—extra clothes and underwear (so much underwear) for every season. Disposable changing pads to line the seats. Wipes, diapers, and enough snacks to feed a desert caravan of camels for three weeks.

But by the end of the day, I can usually count at least five to eight things that did not go as expected and that I wasn't fully prepared for.

Sometimes things can go awry right from the get-go. I remember picking up my youngest from his crib and feeling his hands against my arms as they reached upwards for me. In the dark, I could instantly tell he had a fever, his skin seemingly on fire. Our day would quickly do a one-eighty; from changing activity centers at the library program to changing multiple pull-ups each hour, or from taking in the smells at the local farmers market to a nose raw from bleaching every conceivable surface. I pride myself on my sickness readiness plan. I have the trusty bucket, pull-ups (because even if they're potty trained you can never trust a fart), and a kids medicine basket fully stocked like the wellness aisles of a Walgreens. You will master the pre-vomit warning signs as a stay-at-home mom. I have a fellow mom whose first instinct is to catch the projectile liquid like a freaking baseball. Picturing her gloved up, standing like a little leaguer ready for the big catch, always gives me a good laugh. I prefer to freeze in place until it's all over; it's easier to clean up one spot than a trail to the trash can.

There are lots of other things besides the occasional sickness that can throw your day out of whack. Tantrums that can make you late, a sleeping child who you don't dare wake, or forgetfulness on your part. Like arriving at the store without your grocery list or pulling up to the bank to remember you left your deposit sitting on the kitchen counter with the grocery list. So you decided well at least I can stop by the post office because I did remember the package. Only to swoop into a parking spot and turn around to find your kids sound asleep from all the aimless driving. It's usually at this point I throw my hands up in surrender and go home in defeat. Then, when you think the day can be saved with a few glorious minutes of mommy time while they nap in the car, you recline in the driver's seat to mindlessly scroll Instagram, a child wakes up. Unfortunately, that means the nap schedule is doomed, and probably the rest of the day too, thanks to a very crabby child. And it's only 10 in the morning!

I look back at my former self and laugh. Before kids, I had a plan A. That was it. One plan was all I needed. I was a bit of a perfectionist, so my schedule typically always worked out after overthinking and overplanning. Now I have plans A through Q. Usually, plan C and all those that follow consist of me flying by the seat of my pants because I was not as prepared as I thought. Take one fateful trip to the zoo, for example. The zoo is not just wake-up and "what do you want to do today?" "I dunno, how about a trip to the zoo?" kind of event. Oh no. It's planned, weather patterns tracked, tickets pre-purchased, nearest parking spot to the shuttle scouted, type of event. I drafted up an itinerary, loaded my bags laden with child paraphernalia of every sort, and drove the hour or so to the zoo. It was going to be a glorious day! Little did I know, just not in the way I had intended. Gloriously doomed was more like it.

Child number one couldn't hold it long enough to get to the toilet from the parking lot, even though I offered the car potty about thirty-four times. No problem, bag up the wet bottoms and replace them with fresh ones from the diaper bag. Rinse off the sandals in the sink, and BAM, good to go! Proceed to ooh and ahh at the animals. Child number two does so much ooh-ing and ahh-ing at a passing butterfly (that we could see at home for free, mind you) that they fall and scrape up both knees. No worries, nothing a bandaid and some kisses can't fix. Continue oohing and ahhing only to have the same child spill raspberry snow cone all down the front of their shirt not even five minutes later. Now, child number two is screaming because their knees hurt, they are freezing, sticky, and their special treat is seeping into the pavement along with my will to live. Deep breaths, wipe them down, change their shirt, kiss the knees again, buy another less messy treat. All is calm for about ten blessed minutes. Then, you guessed it, and child number three is up to bat. This child is super upset because they are muddy and soaked due to taking advantage of mom's turned back. At the same time, she was consoling their sibling said child was proceeding to stomp in a large puddle. Child number one is also a mess from joining in on the fun but is very happy about it. To make matters worse, the geese were also frolicking in the same puddle, so I can't be too sure about the true composition of those brown splatters. Either way, the children smell, probably have some weird infection and require a full bath. So what is a mom to do? Visit the newly minted splash pad, of course! About to be christened with its inaugural use as a shower by a somewhat desperate mother.

Success! Sort of, all three children are soaked to the bone. They are cold, wet, tired, and hungry. The 391 snacks I brought plus lunches were not enough for my offspring's insane appetites. My bags of planned perfection are about empty, and I'm done. My patience is gone, I'm sweating to death, and I'm thirsty because the kids emptied my bottle after they used theirs to water a bug. We get to the car, and I strip them down to their birthday suits. At this point, my reserves are running dangerously low. Still, I do have some random clothes and a couple of odd car clothes that have been bouncing around. Everyone is upset and half-naked (aside from me) and yelling, because according to them, "this was the worst day ever!" So much for a fun-filled day at the zoo.

If you're not a go-with-the-flow type of person, you may currently be experiencing sweats and may have had to restrain yourself from pulling out your hair. I feel you. I was a type-A, in charge, handle-it type of woman. To some extent, I still am. But if I didn't learn to roll with the punches, I probably would be writing this book from a padded cell. Knowing to expect the unexpected is vital to your success, not just as a stay-at-home mom but as a parent in general. Your kids will be less stressed, you will be less stressed, and hopefully, there will be less overreacting on your part. I think about when my child spills my freshly poured cup of coffee all over the table or accidentally drops the topless gallon of milk they were pouring. They were trying to be independent and "helpful." If I yell and make a huge deal out of it, my child feels terrible at the moment, and I will undoubtedly feel bad afterward. Again, it was an accident, things happen. It has taken me years to learn how to not freak out in the moment. I still do more than I would like to, but I am a stressed-out mom, so I am allowed a few slips. There have been plenty of times I have dropped, spilled, stepped-on, the list goes on! I'm not perfect, but I find that if I just take the challenges as they come, handling them level-headed and accepting them for what they are (an accident), everyone benefits. My kids experience more of that desired unconditional love, and they gain a sense of security knowing that if they mess up, it isn't the end of the world. Together we can overcome obstacles.

Expecting the unexpected as a stay-at-home mom doesn't have to be related to just your children. Often the idea of what people think a stay-at-home mom does all day and what they do are very different. My husband used to think I didn't do much of anything judging by the state of the house when he arrived home. My working friends think I play with the kids, have plenty of time to complete housework at my leisure, and can swing by Starbucks whenever I want. But neither of these things is true. After just a few weeks as a stay-at-home parent, your understanding of the job description will be nothing like you envisioned. The question isn't what do stay at home moms do all day? It's what *don't* they do all day?

When your kids attempt to make cookies but end up with a viscous dough strong enough to hold together the Eiffel Tower, then they try to hide the evidence by washing it down the sink, you'll magically become a plumber. Of course, being an Uber driver, a referee, and a registered nurse is just par for the course. But you will also get to experience the life of a personal chef, a maid, a scheduling coordinator, a teacher, a financial planner, and hopefully, not a fireman, but there have been times I've been close. Of course, I'm not downplaying the education and demanding jobs of all these exceptional professionals. Still, I hope I am illustrating that a stay-at-home mom must be a jack of all trades. If you don't know how to do something, I guarantee you will quickly learn. I'm impressed with my abilities to unclog a toilet, retrieve a soccer ball from the roof, and single-handedly figure out why my vacuum lost suction. Usually, because someone tried to suck up a three-month-old granola bar that had turned from soft and chewy to the consistency of a rock. Every day will be different, which, admittedly, can get a bit exhausting. However, I think back to a piece of advice I received when I was pregnant with my first child; "you'll never be bored." No more valid words have ever been spoken. I can't even remember the last time I had nothing to do, much less complain about it.

I don't think you can expect the unexpected; that's totally against the definition of unexpected. Instead, do your best to plan for everything and anything to happen, even if it strikes you as being far-fetched. The more ridiculous it seems, the better the chance it will happen. At this point, I don't think I would be surprised if my son told me that he had secretly been keeping a dog in his closet for a month. That aforementioned dog recently had puppies, and now I was required to be a veterinarian, a janitor to clean up the mess in the closet, a dog walker, and a pet store capable of sending the furballs off to loving homes; all while managing to simultaneously keep everyone alive and the house from falling apart. After all, nobody said mommin' was easy.

7

A LUXURY BUT NOT LUXURIOUS

I want to ask you to think about what you might have to give up when becoming a one-income family. What things come to mind? Most certainly elaborate family vacations, probably expensive makeup or home decor items, and likely a pricey cut and color at the salon. What about eating out, getting coffee from a coffee shop, or going to lunch with coworkers? From big to small, your budget will undoubtedly face cuts. However, there are things money can't buy that you will still have to forgo.

For me, one of the most surprising things I had to relinquish was my drive to and from work. Chances are, you, like millions of other drivers, loathe your commute. But when you are suddenly faced without those blessed twenty, thirty, or even sixty minutes of alone time, you'll notice in a big way. I loved getting in my car, being able to blare my music, or listen to a racy podcast; windows slightly down to let the sun warm my face. Just me all by myself with twenty minutes in which all I had to think about was driving. I knew that giving up my job would mean less money, but I don't think I fully realized just how much else I would be giving up too.

It wasn't just the loss of income I struggled with. It was the loss of socialization that hit me the hardest. Sure, the money was nice, but I thrive on social relationships. I need a daily dose of talking to people and listening to their stories, views, and beliefs. Aside from just my friends, I am genuinely fascinated with people. I swear, if you were to look up the definition of people-person in the dictionary, it would have a picture of my face. Now, as a veteran stay-at-home mom, I realize my luxury wasn't being able to grab a venti macchiato on the way to work or purchase tickets to the concert coming to town. It was two much, much simpler things. Talking to adults, and being able to go to the bathroom alone. Two things I believe most people wouldn't even consider an indulgence were what I thought of as spoiling myself. These days I don't even care if it is a public restroom. If you advertise being able to use the toilet without a wide-eyed toddler staring at me and possibly even engaging in a nice bit of chit-chat while washing your hands, I'll be there -- sign me up! What does that say about me as a person? I don't know, but I'm easy to please, okay? Every mom will have a few things that she craves from her former life.

I have found that being a stay-at-home parent works to my advantage in that I hate shopping of any kind. I avoid perusing the clothing aisles like the plague. I will keep pants until I can no longer hide the holes and shirts until I can't disguise the stains. This happens to work well with my current lifestyle as a stay-at-home mom. It also means I didn't feel the loss of a shopping budget as acutely as I felt the absence of other people to talk with.

Though I have a fellow mom who missed the income, spending money was her jam, and there's nothing wrong with that when you have the money to spend! She loved going out to eat, spending an hour or two wandering through boutiques, just buying anything really made her happy. Giving up this lifestyle was a struggle. Once you are confined at home with your children day in and day out, without the means to indulge yourself even a little bit (whether it be in conversation or cappuccinos), that's when the feelings of sadness can set in. Working relationships are snuffed out immediately, like a candle in the wind, friendships fizzle more slowly, like a fire gradually running out of fuel. For a large part of your days and nights, it will be just you and your kids. And don't get me wrong, raising my children is a beautiful experience, and I am grateful for the ability to do so. But that doesn't take away the fact that it can be a mental struggle, giving up so many things that you likely took for granted. Even if the first few weeks or months are a bed of roses, at some point, you will feel the sharp sting of loss. Loss of the old you. It isn't uncommon for stay-at-home moms to think that they've lost their identity. You start out thinking, I'm Marcie Harris, I'll be Marcie Harris even if you pluck me from my office job, set me up with lululemon leggings and a mom bun, and intern me working for demanding tiny humans who think they run the house. Not true. The old you, the one who knew the names of popular bands and the lyrics to their songs, who loved getting dressed up for a night out, who saw movies in the theater that weren't cartoons, may fail to exist for a little while. You might struggle to catch up with all the parts of you that are changing. It's amazing to put the needs of your children and your family before your own, it's a righteous campaign, but that doesn't mean it won't take some getting used to. No longer will you be able to pack your social calendar full, converse with coworkers, or spend a half-hour picking out your outfit, accessories, and doing your hair. As a stay-at-home mom, I'm *less* involved but busier, I don't care about how I look, and I've come to grips with the fact that I have lost some freedoms I once had in a variety of different ways. None of this is terrible, just different. Still, giving up things during this shift was a bit rocky.

I'm not quite sure if it is a good or bad thing, but I am finding that as your children get older, you have less time to think about the old you. At the end of the day, I'm often exhausted, and combined with our tight budget, I have little desire to go out into public and converse with people, much less spend money on a fancy dinner. My hair is always up in a mom bun, so what's the use in coloring it and my clothes will invariably be covered in some unidentifiable substance by noon, so I'm thankful they're not designer. I don't have time to contemplate the latest trends unless I'm researching the latest social media challenge to see if it means my child could permanently damage themselves or their reputation. I am now running all day long, every day. Thankfully, the lack of time to dwell on what your missing is accompanied by more opportunities to meet people in the same season of life as you who are equally focused on their children and their family.

My kids are involved in a host of sports, extracurriculars, and after-school activities. All of these things require them to be driven to and from places, often need volunteers or chaperones, and require a lot of laundry-doing, snack packing, and gear preparation at home. Finding time for the everyday luxuries, ahem, I mean necessities, like eating and bathing, can be difficult. Anything beyond that, like meeting up with a friend, is downright impossible. Becoming friends with other parents who have children in the same activities has become my lifeline. It allows me to socialize with other adults. Not to mention that when my children are out practicing on the field, I can sneak away to go to the bathroom *alone*. Ah, heaven. These are the little things that I find joy in. They have become my luxuries, and while they may not be as grand as the things I once enjoyed, they still lift my spirits and offer me a taste of my former self.

If you find yourself searching for ideas on how to get in touch with the old you or wanting to indulge in the things you once loved, here are a few ways you can do it on a budget.

1. You don't need to don a ballgown, lest you want to end up on the People of Walmart website, but getting a little dressed up once in a while to go grocery shopping can be kind of fun. It makes you feel confident, beautiful, and human again. Sometimes it isn't so much my wardrobe as it is my accessories. I have some great staple pieces of clothing that I rotate and work well

with various shoes, necklaces, and the like for when I'm feeling fancy.

You may be thinking, wait a minute, in previous chapters, you said you hate buying anything new and despise shopping for clothes. This is true. My closet consists of all hand-me-downs (I have told you that I am obsessed with being cheap). I have some excellent Costco plain black leggings and wear them daily during the fall, winter, and spring. They go with everything, and I can move, bend, and sit comfortably. Being able to get on the floor with kids without the fear of your pants splitting is a must. I change it up with a pair of patterned leggings and solid shirts once in a while when I'm feeling spontaneous. My secret for getting dressed up? I have an essential closet but a large jewelry collection. I accessorize my hand-me-down clothes with cheap fashion jewelry. I have a friend who does the same but with purses and another friend that is really into skincare and makeup. Whatever makes you feel like a million bucks, do it. Then go to the store and flaunt your stuff sister!

2. I have mentioned how I used to be very type-A. Part of that was my affinity for keeping things clean and organized. Kids certainly put a wrench in that, but I have found that having my bestie over to help me clean and organize fills my "socialization cup" while also

soothing my perfectionist soul. I put on the movie for the kids, toss a few snacks, and pray that that gives us two hours. Then, we empty a closet, go through cabinets, or sort through drawers. We have fun decluttering and organizing while gabbing away. Some of my very favorite memories were spent cleaning with friends. We laughed so much, mainly at the ridiculous things we found hiding in the back of my closet (Hello pre-kids 90s flare jeans that will never fit my booty again). In the end, you have a happy heart and an organized space.

3. Cook something new each week. For those that love working their magic in the kitchen, trying different recipes can be exciting. Occasionally, you will stumble upon a winner that is not just fun to cook but also approved by your partner and kids. We have found some of our family favorites by trying new recipes off Pinterest. Even if the meal doesn't turn out to be a slam dunk, watching your kids' reaction is a close second. If it is even slightly unrecognizable, meaning it doesn't resemble chicken nuggets or mac n' cheese, mine will usually respond with an overly dramatic "EWWWW," followed by a slow melt out of their seat and down to the floor. It feels like I'm at one of those fancy medieval restaurants where you get dinner and a show!

4. A staycation can be the perfect once in a while splurge. Book a night or two at a local hotel. Try to

schedule it during the week if possible when it is less crowded and is likely to be offering cheaper rates. You can have your partner join you or go solo. Order dinner, swim, and soak in the tub. You can rejoice in knowing that there is no mess to clean up, dishes to do, or activities to run to. Sometimes my whole family comes along, and we've created some extraordinary memories during staycations. My kids love to reminisce about "that one hotel." If you're on a budget, you can pitch a tent in the yard. Falling asleep packed shoulder to shoulder in a hot tent, listening to the sounds of nature, and praying that the pack of coyotes won't find you is not that bad!

5. Join your friends on a Zoom call after you put the kids to sleep. Put on your PJs, grab some wine, and a handful of snacks. Then sign on, relax, chat, and have a great time with your girls. Seeing your friends is way more fun than talking on the phone. And the best part is you don't have to get dressed up, find a sitter, or draw straws for who will be the designated driver. I love the fact that I don't have to worry about squeezing myself into a pair of jeans; after I sign off, I can fall asleep right where I am since I'm already in my pajamas.

6. Indulge in a serene spa night. Put the kids down, fill up the tub, and turn on some soft music. I love to add some relaxing bath salts, and I have been known to

pilfer the garden outside for some fresh rose petals. Give me a good magazine or book, and I'm all set to soak, relax, and unwind.

7. While pedicures and manicures are probably out of the question, there isn't any reason why you can't perform a little TLC at home. My daughter and I love soaking our feet in the tub, and occasionally I can convince her that I'll give her a foot massage if she gives me one. Then we spread out all our nail polish and paint our toes. It's an inexpensive way to pamper ourselves while also getting in some much-needed one on one time.

8. If you really enjoy shopping, you could consider becoming a couponer. Hunting for a good deal this way will allow you to shop without breaking the budget. One of my friends loves to see how much she can save or what things she can get for free. It may appear as a bit of an obsession to an outsider, but she swears it's her therapy. I don't have the patience, but I do love the deals she shares. Sometimes she will even act as my personal shopper. I don't have to leave the house, and she enjoys the excuse to get out and hit the stores; it's a win-win.

I've heard the phrase, "being a stay-at-home mom is a luxury, but it's not luxurious." Isn't that the truth? I'm grateful to be able to stay home with my kiddos, but I sometimes still mourn the person I used to be and the freedoms I used to have. Losing your income and some of the things you indulge in, maybe even without realizing it, is challenging, but there are definitely ways to make it manageable. When all else fails, I turn to my trusty support system. I quickly send a "tell me I'm pretty" text to the group, and they'll go above and beyond to make sure I feel beautiful. Tired eyes, oatmeal-crusted hair, milk-stained shirt, holey-leggings and all.

8

MOM GUILT

I conducted an informal survey of moms who work outside of the home and those that stay home. It centered around issues they struggle with concerning their children and their work-life balance, and all the emotions stemming from them. Do you know what the number one problem both groups of moms cited? Mom guilt.

It seems like from the time your little wet raisin of a baby is placed in your arms; you become susceptible to mom guilt. When they're young, we agonize over letting them cry in their crib or deciding to bottle feed instead of breastfeeding. Then, as they get older, it becomes guilt over food choices and screen time. Unfortunately, mom guilt never goes away, and like a disease, it can spread into every motherly decision you make if you let it.

It isn't hard to see where working mothers' mom guilt stems from. They feel the weight of their decision to work outside the home and have someone else watch their children. In some cases, this is the best scenario for their sanity, their family's budget and doesn't negatively affect their kiddos. Nevertheless, they wonder if they are making the right decision each time they drop their little ones off at daycare. But stay-at-home moms aren't immune to guilt.

Mom guilt hits them a bit differently. When you become a stay-at-home mom, you are the one tasked with caring for your children, teaching your children, providing them with social experiences, enriching their lives on a daily, etc. That's a lot of pressure! I often felt guilty when I rolled into bed, exhausted and drained, and only to remember that I didn't play an educational game, or perform a learning activity, or do anything pertaining to school-based instruction during the day. Were my kids failing, was I neglecting their knowledge and development, were they destined to be forever behind because mom let them watch Paw Patrol instead of practicing their ABCs?! The truth is, probably not. One or two days of missed educational curriculum and learning games wouldn't doom my kids, but it didn't feel that way.

I have learned that many of the things we moms do and say throughout the day can be highly educational for our children. We can be incredible teachers just by narrating our activities and turning everyday life moments into learning opportunities. Did you know your kids can learn their colors from you telling them the name of each M&M they are eating just as well as if you sat them down and did flashcards? Their kindergarten teacher isn't going to care if they grasped the concept of counting to twenty from counting the amount of loose goldfish and tampons in the bottom of your purse or using actual mathematical counters. I'm not advocating that you forgo evidence-based activities or tried and true learning games altogether, but you don't need to beat yourself up if you skip a day or two. Our kids are like tiny sponges, soaking up every ounce of information all day long, which is an important thing to remember when you step on a lego for the tenth time that day and are about to let loose. They can learn a lot from watching, listening, and interacting with you.

It isn't all about teaching them letters or numbers either. To be happy, fulfilled, and well-adjusted adults, I believe my kids need to learn life skills, practical knowledge, problem-solving strategies, and a whole host of things that rote memorization and contextualized learning won't teach them. So I engage with them in make-believe play, explore outside, and generally follow their lead about what they are interested in. All the while, they are picking up new concepts, skills, and strategies that will hopefully make them a better human, not just an all "A" student. So why should I feel guilty about doing these things instead of sitting them down with a worksheet? I shouldn't. But now and again, the mom guilt creeps in. Like, when I need to keep the kids occupied with the TV for an hour. But I take a deep breath and remind myself that if I don't meet with my therapist on Zoom, I may lose it, making me feel guilty. Then I turn on the subtitles so I feel better about them watching Bluey for the hundredth time. Research shows that turning on the subtitles while children are watching TV can improve reading skills and comprehension. So don't feel too bad.

Mom guilt rears its ugly head in other ways too. Like when I talk to fellow moms and hear how their children are in a weekly library group, on a dance team, and take Spanish lessons every Tuesday. Meanwhile, my toddler can belt out the lyrics to Billy Joel's "Just the Way You Are" but can't recite the Itsy Bitsy Spider. The only Spanish they know is from Dora the Explorer, and I'm guessing family dance parties in our living room do not count as being on a dance team. I'm here to tell you that those things are great, wonderful, fantastic! My kiddo does take swim lessons and attend library events now and again too. But just because you are with your kids all day doesn't mean you have to do "kids things" 24/7. You're a human, just as your child is, and it's okay to have interests and preferences outside of your children. Even if you don't devote every waking moment to developmentally appropriate lessons, crafts, and outings, you're a great parent. I think my kid will thank me for his expansive musical knowledge one day and fondly recall pushing the living room couch and chairs out of the way to jump around to Billy Joel with his mom.

I've also felt blameworthy when I haven't wanted to play with my kids. I can't be the only one that does not love playing tea parties or race cars with my kids all the time, right? My daughter often sits me down with her dolls for a live reenactment of a Barbie episode she just saw, and I find myself nodding off while Ken takes a rest in the Dreamhouse. Then I inevitably hear, "No mommy! It is NOT nap time! It is time for school! Now, get up!". My playing often fails to meet her expectations miserably, going something like this: Fine. "Can my doll go on vacation?" "No mommy, she has to go to school!" "My doll does not like to follow the rules." "MOMMY! That's not how you play! You are terrible at this! I'm not playing with you!" "Okay then. How about we play hide and seek, you hide and wait for me to find you?" "No mommy, last time you took a million years to find me and it was boring."

Little did she know that I was the one doing the hiding, eating cookies in peace. Do I feel like a terrible mother because of this? Absolutely. However, I try to make up for it in other ways, like taking them to their favorite park or going on a nature hike (one of their most loved activities). I don't just focus on what I see as my failures, but I reflect on all the times I made my children laugh, smile, or the special moments we enjoyed. It's the little things, a few minutes of cuddling or a short-lived tickle match, that add up and hopefully outweigh the times when my Barbie playing abilities weren't up to par.

You already know that I love being frugal. While saving money typically makes me elated, I have found myself feeling guilty because my children often are dressed in hand-me-downs (great looking and gently used hand-me-downs mind you), and not the name-brand fresh-off-the-rack clothes that some of their peers wear. However, I know that budgeting and saving money is what's best for our family. I also understand that these topics are good life lessons to learn. There will always be people who have more than them and people who have less too. Being able to afford things takes work and effort, and when you have what you need, you shouldn't forget to be generous with others. My children may not understand this or *want* to understand this when they're the ones ogling over the latest ripped pair of fashion jeans that we could never afford. Still, I feel less guilty knowing that my frugality is investing in their future in more ways than one.

Maybe you feel guilty when you look around your house and see all the clutter and the mess despite your efforts to keep everything tidy. That is normal. My kids can destroy every room in the house in as little as two hours, while it takes me at least two hours to put just one room back together after they've blown through. Some days it seems like it's impossible to raise kids and have a clean house. You have to choose one. You can't have both. And don't even get me started on the yard. I remember pre-kids driving past homes where their front lawn looked like the house had thrown up on it; bikes, plastic playhouses, toys littered the yard. I naively thought, "Who could live like that?". It turns out it's a sleep-deprived mom who's too busy with trying to keep the inside of the house clean, her kids fed and educated, and her shit together; that's who. My yard usually gets a nightly pick-up and a weekly deep clean when the children dash around desperately trying to save their stuff from the lawnmower. Other than that, it's a minefield; enter at your own risk.

The one area we do have landscaped hasn't faired much better. The dog frequently digs up the plants, my free-ranging horde of chickens inflicts chaos upon the mulch, and my poor potted plants have been deprived of water for far too long. It has taken me years to realize that sometimes it's better to just shut the doors than to try and keep up with the yard work. Snuggling up for naps and watching cartoons is way more fun.

The guilt I have because I don't have anything left for my partner often plagues me. By the time I go to bed, I am mentally, physically, and emotionally drained. If one more person touches me or talks to me, I'm going to lose my mind. As soon as the kids are down for the night, I retreat to the bedroom, hoping for just a few minutes to read a book, scroll social media, or maybe catch half a tv episode before my eyelids droop closed. Then in walks my husband. "Hey honey, you look tired. Want me to rub your back?" If it's that kind of touching, I'll take it, "Yes, that would be wonderful!" Finally, he gets it! After about three minutes, as the knots are just starting to relax, his hands begin wandering to my boobs, and I feel something poking my leg. Seriously?! Here I am at 10:00 pm, expected to please yet another person when I was just hoping for a brief respite! Then I feel guilty because he has been working all day to provide for our family. I should be honored to know that he is still attracted to me in that way, and our marriage should be just as important as our focus on our children. So, I did what any good wife would do and made him give me a relaxing non-sensual massage for thirty minutes before I finally gave in. That fulfilled my good wife quota for the week.

Yelling and screaming can really bring on remorse. This eats at my soul daily. I am ashamed to admit that I am a yeller. I could never fathom spanking my children, so I yell. Some days I yell often. There are days when I am on a constant loop of repeating myself, punctuated by bouts of screaming what I just said for what seems like the hundredth time. It isn't unheard of for me to answer my kids' questions in the form of a yell. The poor unsuspecting individuals on the other end of my phone calls probably think I have a hearing problem because I subconsciously yell at them as well. In my defense, I did work at a nursing home right before I became a mother, and my husband is partially deaf from being around heavy machinery all his life. I got into the habit of yelling before my kids made it a lifestyle. Yelling is like showering. If you don't do it, no one will listen to you.

I have no shame in admitting that I'm not a calm person by nature. I live in a perpetual state of frazzled. But even though my force field of chaos, I have noticed that genuinely calm people don't seem to yell as much. It's probably because they have calm kids who don't require yelling; at least, that's what I tell myself to feel better. I have no solution to not yelling. It works for us, so I do it. I feel bad about it, but I still do it.

Guilt and the holidays seem to go hand in hand, don't they? I'm not talking about indulging in too many Christmas cookies or spending too much on gifts. I'm talking about feeling guilty because you don't always have time for non-immediate family. It doesn't even have to be solely at Christmas, Hanukkah, or Easter, but just regularly getting together for a visit. This hits me the hardest. I have always tried to make time for my family and be present for all parties, dinners, and gatherings. I genuinely love my family, and I enjoy being there for them. Lately, though, it seems impossible. There is little time for anything else between the kids having daily activities and me trying to accomplish things at the house. It doesn't help that my family doesn't have any young kids, so gatherings are rough because they are usually not kid-friendly. Let me tell you if you don't have kids, or your kids are no longer little, you don't understand how much effort it takes to attend an event with small children. It is A LOT of work to plan for every conceivable situation concerning keeping them entertained and fed. I have to bring snacks and meal alternatives if my relatives are trying to serve foie gras to a five-year-old. I pack practically an entire toy box to prevent them from going after the glass sculptures and rare art conveniently displayed at toddler eye level. When we have to travel to someone else's home, my anxiety goes through the roof. OCD runs in my family, so their abodes are usually pristine both inside and out. There are knick-knacks, priceless valuables, choking hazards, and white things around every corner. So many white things. I am constantly panicking because my kids are tornadoes and usually leave a path of destruction behind them. It's not fun. My kids are miserable because I'm constantly hounding them for every little thing, and I'm miserable because I can't relax and enjoy my family. God forbid one of my kids' sneezes or coughs, then it's game over. Everyone goes into germaphobe mode and keeps their distance. The guilt comes over me in waves, and I'm thinking, crap, now I feel bad if one of my kids is getting sick and I just brought them here. I hope my family knows that if I had any inclination my child was sick, I wouldn't have brought them—anxiety overload. In short, the only time I can spend with my family is at my house, and finding the time to plan a cookout or dinner is in short supply nine months out of the year when school and extracurriculars are in session.

My husband's family is easier to be with because we all have kids the same age, and my husband is one of five. Things are far from perfect. Having anything white might as well be taboo, and we fit right in. The downside is they all live far away, and each of us is heavily involved in sports and activities. This means we're in short supply of both times to visit and money in the budget to get there. In a perfect world, I would live in an RV with a potted money tree and travel around visiting all my family and friends. I would be able to watch my nieces and nephews grow older. I would be able to have my parents and grandparents be a part of my kids' lives. Let them watch my children grow and experience new wonders each day. Sadly, that is not my reality, and I deal with extreme amounts of guilt because of it. I hope that adding a monthly gathering to my schedule might help will it into fruition.

All this guilt can manifest in weird ways. For example, as a young mother, I would not only find myself feeling guilty about not playing with my kids enough or going to see my family but also anxious about the physical act of doing some of these things. I would feel incredibly anxious about leaving the house.

Anxiety is a funny thing. Growing up, I never knew that I suffered from anxiety. It was masked by the fact that I was always the center of attention and the child who was up for anything—eternally on the go, experiencing life and trying everything. I was social, adventurous, happy-go-lucky, ready to live. Looking back, I definitely battled with anxiety and was oblivious because it wasn't indeed a thing back then. Anything that could be perceived as a sign of weakness was never discussed. I grew up in what I refer to as the Pepto Bismal Era, where everything was determined to be a result of "irritable bowel syndrome," and those afflicted were prescribed a stomach remedy. Butterflies in your stomach? IBS. Have the nervous shits every day? IBS. Get stomach aches every time you are in a new environment? IBS. Have a hard time breathing, headache, and stomach pains? *It definitely* sounds like IBS. Nothing was attributed to anxiety.

But things finally became very, very apparent after I had my first child. I had terrible panic attacks almost every time I left the house—scary panic attacks. The ones where you can't breathe and your world is spinning, and you are on the verge of passing out any second. Seeing stars would have been nice compared to the pure white that would cloud my vision during these episodes. So I kept ignoring it while tossing back shots of the pink stuff.

My OCD played a significant role in my anxiety. It was getting to the point that I couldn't leave my house unless it was perfect. All the dishes had to be done, and the counters cleared before I could even think about my next move. We were always late for everything. If I did leave the house out of sorts, it would run through my mind; bugging me and making it impossible to focus on anything else. All I could think about was getting back home so I could finish what I started. I was going through life with what felt like the weight of the world on my chest. Every single day I felt like I was suffocating with no end in sight. My to-do list kept doubling hourly, and no matter what I did, I could never seem to catch up. Finally, a close friend said, "Girl, you need meds!" I laughed and said, "no way." I'm a very stubborn person and have been doing fine for years. However, when I started to think about my fixation with keeping my house perfect and the fear that gripped me, should I have to leave my house in a state of perfectness, along with the other women in my family (here's looking at you "obsessed" aunt Pat); I realized my friend might just be right. I always thought I could manage it on my own. If I could get ahead of the game, things would be easier; I would keep up then. After being behind daily for years, I realized that I couldn't live up to the standard of perfection I had for myself. So, I saw my doctor. Being diagnosed with OCD was a life changer. Now I'm free. I am not entirely rid of my anxiety but free from the paralyzing feelings resulting from my OCD.

I know how to use the right strategies to not only function but enjoy life! I'm not suggesting you run out and get a prescription. But I suggest that you take a minute and try to identify the root of your anxiety and guilt. Try and figure out your triggers, talk to your family or your bestie and see if they notice any patterns. Most women have a flare-up of anxiety after the birth of their child. Remember being afraid to go to sleep because what if your newborn stopped breathing? We've all been there. But if your anxiety has persisted and is restricting you from happily experiencing life, see your doctor.

How does the age-old adage go? According to Benjamin Franklin, the only thing for certain in life is death and taxes? Well, I think we need to add mom guilt to that list. I'm convinced that it will always be there, sneaking up when we least expect it. After all, raising kids right puts parents under a lot of pressure. When we're not worrying about feeding them the baby cereal that isn't dairy-free, organic, non-GMO, and picked and processed by the hand of God himself, we will be obsessing over if that time we yelled at them to grow up and act mature (seeing as they're a teenager now), may have messed them up for life. Whether our guilt is temporary or long-term, the ideals set forth by society and social media especially don't make things easy on us. That's why we have to be gentle with ourselves and other mamas. Surround yourself with others who listen to you, support you, and tell you you're a good mom.

Trust your mama instincts and know you're doing your best to raise your kids. Most importantly, just love on them. I adore the quote by Jill Churchill, "There is no way to be a perfect mother and a million ways to be a good one." Don't listen to the voice telling you you're not good enough; you're doing great mama!

9

FAILED IT?

When you're in the workforce, it's often easy to measure your success. You have deadlines and due dates, you can track data on spreadsheets, and there's always the oh-so-wonderful feedback from your boss. But as a stay-at-home mom, it can be challenging to know if you are succeeding or struggling. More often than not, this uncertainty can lead to you feeling like a failure.

When I was pregnant, aka "the most perfect mom ever," I thought that I could handle this stay-at-home-mom thing. I am very type-A, remember, so when it came to my work, I was always on top of my game, meeting quotas, getting great reports, the whole deal. How hard could it be to totally rock being a stay-at-home mom when I only had to report to a tiny infant? This baby and my husband would be the only two people grading my efforts, and one of them couldn't even wipe their own behind. I was convinced that this would be a piece of cake; the baby would be well-cared for, the house would be spotless, and I might even pick up some new cooking skills.

Flash forward to a couple of weeks after giving birth. I was scoring "satisfactory" in only one of those three areas. The baby was well taken care of, even if it was a bit of trial and error some days (swaddle sacks and baby carriers can be tricky), at least I was meeting one goal. But the house was a disaster, my cooking most definitely did not improve, and I began to doubt being a stay-at-home mom. Why wasn't this more manageable for me? Why wasn't I "good" at it? Aren't we women supposed to know how to be a mom naturally? Isn't it like, ingrained into our DNA or something?

Throw in a few more years and a few more kids, and things improved a little. But it's just more clothes to wash, mouths to feed, and toys to pick up. So most days, the bathrooms didn't get cleaned, and the living room was a mess, and at least one person complained about my inferior culinary skills. If I think about it too hard and for too long, I realize that I've felt like a failure during the majority of my days as a stay-at-home mom.

I probably shouldn't have yelled at my child. I probably shouldn't have let them eat marshmallows instead of carrot sticks. I probably should've changed out of the yoga pants that haven't slid off my body in three days straight. I probably should've put away laundry during naptime instead of scrolling on my phone. My list of "failures" is long. But the best way I have found to overcome these feelings of inadequacy is to change my perspective.

It's all about how you look at things. First, I remind myself that I am a stay-at-home mom. I am not a stay-at-home mom/chef/maid/Uber driver/teacher/supermodel. All of those things may be in my job description eventually, but first and foremost, my duty is to my children. Speaking of which, take a step back and look at how hard the job of being a stay-at-home mom truly is. You never get breaks, pay, or even a "good job." I would never work for a company for free, around the clock, without guaranteed breaks. Especially one where the bosses frequently tell me that they don't like me and I'm doing everything wrong. All while being expected to supervise other employees who always seem to loathe one another unless they're in cahoots to push the boundaries and break the rules. Yet, here I am. Listening to a pint-sized CEO yell and scream that it is my fault that he dropped his plate of eggs on the floor.

But for all its difficulty, it is also incredibly rewarding. So rewarding, I can't think of another career like it.

Just as we worked on changing our pros to cons earlier in this book, try to change your attitude and mindset. I like to rephrase my "have to's" to "gets," which isn't always easy. For example, I don't "have to" take my kids to gymnastics lessons; I "get to" take them when most parents can't due to work, hectic schedules, or lessons not being within the budget. I don't "have to" make breakfast for my kids; I "get to" when other moms and dads are busy trying to rush out the door for their own busy day. We get to experience these things while raising our children, something we shouldn't take for granted. I was present when my kids said their first word and took their first steps. I get to love on them and kiss them whenever I want. It isn't always easy, or perfect, or ideal. Still, I try and remind myself that this isn't an opportunity afforded to everyone. The other mindset I am actively working on changing is what the stereotypical perfect stay-at-home-mom looks like. For me, it's someone who has it all together without looking like she tries too hard. Her mom bun is perfectly casual, with coiffed flyaways framing her face like a halo. She can make an oversized sweatshirt and leggings look like they belong on the runway. Her house is Instagram-ready, her schedule is brimming with child-friendly and developmentally stimulating activities, and her kids never put up a fuss. Though you can bet if they did, she would calmly reason with them until they reached a loving, mutual understanding. This is the mom I feel like I never measure up to. But in the words of my daughter's ice queen idol, I need to LET IT GO!

Because you know what? In your child's mind, you are the perfect mom (most days). I mean, when they're young and with you day in and day out, they don't have much of a frame of reference, so feel free to be you. You don't need Instagram-perfect photos; my favorite picture of my kids is when I found them skinny dipping in the mud pit that had formed overnight in our yard. I literally had to grit my teeth and reach into the suspicious murk to fish their mud-caked undies from the bottom. Your home doesn't have to be Better Homes & Gardens decorated. If decorating is your jam, do it, but do it for you, not anyone else. You don't need Pinterest-ready party favors for every occasion. Just because you are a stay-at-home doesn't mean you have endless amounts of time, the will, or the desire to be whatever version of an ideal mother you have created in your mind.

You can have all the schedules, routines, budgets, and checklists you want; unfortunately, you will still fail some days. By this point, you should know I love my schedules and routines. I have a planner devoted to organizing activities, meal plans, and more. But every now and then, the universe seems to notice that things are going absolutely swimmingly in our household and decides to throw a wrench in the plan. Like when we were driving to our weekly grocery shopping adventure, our car got a very sudden and very explosive flat tire. There I was, three kids in tow, on the side of the road trying to remember exactly where the spare tire was located. As I struggled to remove my flat tire while keeping up the charade of a positive attitude for my children, someone pulled over to help (much to my delight!). Unfortunately, while trying to assist this good samaritan with the tire change, my children are very loudly and obviously melting down inside the vehicle. I did my best to scold them with empty threats under my breath so I wouldn't sound like a complete psycho, combined with throwing food at them like animals in a petting zoo in the hopes that they stop shrieking. Finally, the tire was changed, and we headed off to the repair shop. The lovely gentleman wished me luck, because of course, "I looked like I had my hands full." But luck wasn't on our side. Hours later, we limped home, no groceries, a blown budget, and on the brink of a breakdown due to missed naps and lunch. Not only was my day in shambles, but I felt as if it had completely thrown off my week. Looking back, I think the terrible times helped me appreciate the effort I put into creating a good schedule and routine that keeps our family happily functioning.

I have no shame in admitting, though, that some days I give up before the day even begins. After a particularly rough night the following day, I might decide, screw the schedule. Instead, I head to the couch, coffee in hand, and decide that I might as well chalk this day up to a failure before even trying. I don't care how big of a mess the kids make or if they eat cereal for breakfast, lunch, and dinner. I take a day off from being the micromanaging mom and tell myself tomorrow is a fresh start.

I feel like I eventually made peace with myself, my goals, and what I believed failure and perfection looked like as a stay-at-home mom. So what's a (finally) content and self-loving gal to do? Try her hand at something else high-stakes that could undoubtedly result in feelings of failure, of course!

After my children got a bit older, I thought for sure I would be able to go back to work full-time. By now, I had got this mom-thing down. I was no longer naive. I was a seasoned veteran of motherhood. Additionally, I had previously been a working woman. I felt confident in both areas, so why shouldn't I be able to handle being a working mom? For all my bravado, I was so nervous that updating my resume took me a couple of weeks. I was convinced that no one would want to hire me due to the gap in my work history and the glaring lack of recent work experience. What did I have to offer in the way of skills? I could nurse a baby while cooking dinner and simultaneously mopping up a mess with my foot. Still, I doubted any company would require that particular skill set. I knew how dedicated, resourceful, and responsible I was as an employee, but on paper, I seemed underqualified and out of date. I was in shock when I was offered a full-time position as an office administrator.

To say I was excited to rejoin the adult world was an understatement. I was so damn excited it was giving me anxiety about if my level of excitement was normal. At that point, I hadn't cared where I was offered a job, as long as there were other adults there with me. But an office administrator position was better than I could have hoped for! I guess multitasking is a pretty good quality to have, and I feel like stay-at-home moms are the top dog of multitaskers. Maybe the HR person was a former stay-at-home mom herself, and perhaps they emailed the wrong candidate. I didn't *care*; I was about to have my solo car rides back! Possible opportunities to chat with others in the breakroom and goals that didn't involve trying to keep the dog glitter and glue-free for more than two hours.

I started within a week, and let me tell you, that was a very stressful week. My fears and anxiety were on overload. I was terrified of failing my first attempt at getting back out into the workforce. Still, I pushed through and thought I had everything planned out perfectly. I have a wonderful friend that agreed to watch my children for the rest of the summer until school starts at an on-budget rate. I had my kids taken care of, meals planned, business slacks and heels at the ready, I was set! For the first couple of weeks, I was on cloud nine. I was so ecstatic to be back at work. My routine was gelling, my boss loved me and my work ethic, my kids were doing fine, our budget was finally in the black, and even my husband seemed more cheerful. I was happy. Then the universe struck again. My three-month job anniversary and the COVID-19 shutdown walked onto the scene hand in hand.

Things started to get a bit more challenging. Fall approached, and remote learning was in full swing. Unfortunately, my sitter nor I were prepared for the nightmare that was about to come. Remote learning was going about as well as, well I can't even think of anything to compare it to. It was horrible. That's all I got. My children and her children are all in elementary school. Having numerous children in separate rooms while streaming their "classes" was a little like running a marathon in a small building while tiny children yelled at you for help all at the same time. There are no skills or classes to prepare you for this. Soon enough, my sitter was completely burnt out, and so was I. Trying to work and getting phone calls from my sitter, asking questions about my kids' classes. At the same time, I could hear the whining and arguments in the background, which made my anxiety skyrocket. I could tell my babysitter was trying her hardest, but as her best friend, I could hear the desperation in her voice.

Eventually, I said goodbye to my job. I tapped out. The practices being put into place at the company I worked for stressed me out. All of my children attending school remotely stressed me out. I was miserable, and they were miserable. In a cruel and ironic twist of fate, my children, who once had told me, "why can't you just get a job like other moms so we can go to a babysitter!?" "We hate being home all the time with you! This is so boring!" now cried every morning, "Why did you get a job?" "I just want to stay home for once!" As they say, you can't please everyone all the time; although I'm pretty sure the saying should go something like "you can't please your children...ever".

At the time, in my mind, this was a massive fail for me. Epic. Even though Covid was ultimately to blame, I still felt like I could have done things differently. I felt like I could have handled things better or just pushed aside my opinions about the company I worked for. There are thousands of people in my position, and they make it work. They go to work every day, so should I. I made it six months. The emotional rollercoaster that came afterward was a struggle. My identity of something other than just a "mom" was stripped away, again. I saw friends and other women still succeeding in the business world, achieving the professional fulfillment I had so briefly tasted. Now all that was left was a bitter taste.

It's a hard place to be in because my kids wanted me home. I knew that being able to help them with their online schooling would ultimately be better for them, my friend who no longer had to babysit, and her children who also were learning remotely. But what about me? There were times I felt that I resented my children. Then I felt horrible for resenting my kids who just wanted their *mom.* How selfish could I be? I flipped-flopped between grateful and gutted. It was like I was starting back at the beginning, trying to find my place all over again.

Talk about starting over; I wish I had a copy of this book then! It took me a couple of months to get back into my stay-at-home mom routine, take my own advice, and wait for the feelings of ultimate failure to recede. Finally, I realized that doing a complete one-eighty and diving head-first into full-time employment was probably not the best decision. While I probably could have made it work sans-Covid, it wasn't the greatest transition for my children. I wanted so badly to be my former self again that I failed to consider the fact that the old me did not have three kids. If the epiphany that I will never be who I was again was a sudden deep breath in, the realization that I'm okay with that was a slow and controlled exhale of relief. Life indeed isn't a straight path, but there are no loops back to the past. It's an adventure of twists and turns with a learning experience around every corner. Without failure, there would be no growth.

Eventually, the universe dropped another opportunity into my lap that couldn't be more perfect for my family. I teach at a preschool now. This lets me have lots of time with my children while also getting out of the house for a few hours each day, reclaiming some of my identity while also getting the immense satisfaction of teaching and shaping young minds. Do I find my profession slightly ironic, considering I once struggled with staying home with my kids day in and day out? Yes. But being involved in the lives of children, whether your own or entrusted to you, is one of the most rewarding things I have ever done. And so, in this phase of life, I am happy. I am at peace. Will this contentment last forever? I hope not. What's life without a bit of adversity and challenge? I don't regret my decision to become a stay-at-home mom, nor do I regret my decision to try and work full-time once again. When that door slammed in my face, I found my way to a wide-open window that led to the perfect job for my family and me. I encourage you to embrace the stage of life you are in, whether it be wiping noses and changing diapers all day or trying to find your way back into the workforce. Though the days may feel long, they don't last forever. So soak up every ounce of the magic and madness of motherhood while you can.

I would love it if you could take a minute to leave me an honest review on Amazon. Reviews help me grow as a writer and help Amazon weed out poor-quality scam books. I hope my book helped you in some way. I hope you laughed at my mom failures and gained some reassurance that you are not alone in this crazy mayhem we call parenting.

Make sure you join my Facebook group "MOMs aka Mayors of Mayhem" by scanning the QR code below, to hear more mom fails and survival tips from lots of fellow parents working on managing the daily mayhem.

A FREE GIFT FOR MY READERS!

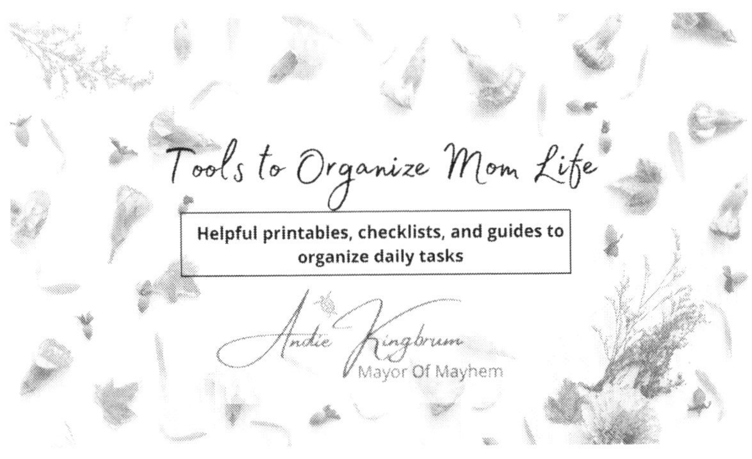

TEN downloadable pages to help fellow parents get organized in daily life. Scan the QR code below to receive your FREE printable tools.

https://themayorofmayhem.activehosted.com/f/1

REFERENCES

Leonhardt, M. (2020, January 27). *Parents are spending $42 billion on early child care - that's more than federal and state spending combined*. CNBC. Retrieved November 12, 2021, from https://www.cnbc.com/2020/01/27/parents-spending-42-billion-on-early-child-care-each-year.html.

Moran, P. (2021, November 12). *How much is a homemaker worth?* Investopedia. Retrieved November 12, 2021, from https://www.investopedia.com/financial-edge/0112/how-much-is-a-homemaker-worth.aspx.

Elizabeth Mendes, L. S. and K. M. G. (2021, August 25). *Stay-at-home moms report more depression, sadness, anger*. Gallup.com. Retrieved November 12, 2021, from https://news.gallup.com/poll/154685/Stay-Home-Moms-Report-Depression-Sadness-Anger.aspx.

Bennett, S. (2021, July 16). *Do I have the baby blues or postpartum depression?* American Pregnancy Association. Retrieved November 12, 2021, from https://americanpregnancy.org/healthy-pregnancy/first-year-of-life/baby-blues-or-postpartum-depression/.

NOTES

1. THE PROS AND CONS OF BEING A STAY-AT-HOME MOM

1. https://www.cnbc.com/2020/01/27/parents-spending-42-billion-on-early-child-care-each-year.html

3. THE GRASS IS ALWAYS GREENER - TRANSITIONING WITH YOUR PARTNERS FULL SUPPORT

1. How Much Is A Homemaker Worth? (investopedia.com)

4. FAMILY, FRIENDS, AND FELLOW DOMESTIC ENGINEERS - BUILDING YOUR SUPPORT SYSTEM

1. https://news.gallup.com/poll/154685/stay-home-moms-report-depression-sadness-anger.aspx
2. ,(https://americanpregnancy.org/healthy-pregnancy/first-year-of-life/baby-blues-or-postpartum-depression/)

Made in United States
Orlando, FL
26 June 2022

19177644R00098